CONNAUGHT

TRAVEL GUIDE

LANZAROTE

D0785982

ROWLAND MEAD

★★★ Highly recommended
★★ Recommended
★ See if you can

This edition is published by Connaught
an imprint of New Holland Publishers Ltd
London • Cape Town • Sydney • Auckland
First published in MMIII
10 9 8 7 6 5 4 3 2 1

website: www.newhollandpublishers.com

Garfield House, 86 Edgware Road
London W2 2EA, United Kingdom

80 McKenzie Street
Cape Town 8001, South Africa

14 Aquatic Drive, Frenchs Forest,
NSW 2086, Australia

218 Lake Road, Northcote,
Auckland, New Zealand

Publishing Manager (UK): Simon Pooley
Publishing Manager (SA): Thea Grobbelaar
DTP Cartographic Manager: Genené Hart

Editors: Jacqueline de Villiers and Melany
McCallum
Picture Researcher: Colleen Abrahams
Design and DTP: Lellyn Creamer
Cartographer: Marisa Galloway
Proofreader: Thea Grobbelaar
Reproduction by Hirt & Carter (Pty) Ltd, Cape Town
Printed and bound by Times Offset (M) Sdn. Bhd.,
Malaysia.

Cover Photographs
Top Left: *Ginés, with the white houses of Arrecife on
the shore.* **Top Right:** *Mancha Blanca's church, the
Ermita de los Dolores, was threatened by encroaching
lava in 1824.* **Bottom Left:** *Dancers in local costume
at a festival in Teguise.* **Bottom Right:** *The resort of
Playa Blanca is backed by a red volcanic cone.*

Title Page: *A young lady in traditional costume takes
part in a festival at Teguise.*

CONTENTS

1
Introducing Lanzarote

Lanzarote, the most easterly island in the Canary archipelago, is in many ways unique. Although all the islands are volcanic, it is on Lanzarote that the volcanic features are most impressive and easily approachable. It is possible to take a bus right to the very top of a volcano that, geologically speaking, has recently erupted and, an hour later, travel over low hills of volcanic ash and cinder on a camel. Within a few kilometres of these 'mountains of fire' there are pretty villages of whitewashed houses, which are surrounded by vines growing in sheltered hollows in the volcanic cinders.

Although all of the Canary Islands have pleasant winter weather, it is Lanzarote that has the most consistent climate. Since it is situated close to Africa with no high mountains, Lanzarote has more sunshine than any other of the islands. Daytime temperatures in January and February are rarely below 22°C (72°F), and rainfall is light and falls on no more than 16 days a year. Not surprisingly, Lanzarote has become a popular winter holiday destination for northern Europeans. They are attracted to the climate and the harmonious nature of the landscape, which is not as developed as the other islands.

César Manrique – artist, sculptor and environmentalist – wielded an enormous influence over Lanzarote's government and is largely responsible for preserving the island's natural state. He was well aware of the destructive consequences that tourism can bring and was determined to keep the island from being spoiled. As a result, nearly two-thirds of Lanzarote is free from tourist

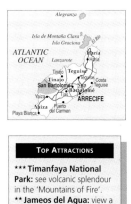

Top Attractions

*** Timanfaya National Park: see volcanic splendour in the 'Mountains of Fire'.
** Jameos del Agua: view a partly collapsed volcanic tube, with a subterranean lake.
** Cueva de los Verdes: take a 2km (1.2-mile) guided walk through a lava cave.
** Mirador del Río: clifftop viewpoint and restaurant overlooking Isla Graciosa.
* Teguise: see elegant buildings and a vibrant Sunday market in the former capital.
* Fundación César Manrique: visit an art gallery in Manrique's former home.

Opposite: *An artificial geyser in Timanfaya National Park.*

establishments and where development has taken place, respect for local customs and traditions is evident. Manrique's influence can be seen everywhere, from roadside sculptures to restaurants that blend harmoniously into volcanic lava. No building is taller than a Canary palm tree and roadside hoardings are banned.

The unique combination of the mild temperature, well-preserved landscape and the might of the volcanoes is appealing to discriminating tourists and many return year after year. The number of British tourists alone increased from 43,000 in 1982 to nearly three-quarters of a million at the turn of the century. Visitors always receive a warm welcome from the *Lanzaroteños*, who have managed to accommodate mass tourism without sacrificing their heritage.

THE LAND

Lanzarote is one of the **Canary Islands**, an archipelago lying approximately 300km (186 miles) west of the African coast of Morocco. The islands belong to Spain, which is 1120km (696 miles) to the northeast. Lanzarote lies on latitude 28° north, some 480km (298 miles) from the Tropic of Cancer. It is about 60km (37 miles) long and 21km (13 miles) wide at its broadest point, covering some 813km² (314 square miles). In addition to Lanzarote, there are six other islands in the archipelago – Tenerife, Gran Canaria, La Palma, Fuerteventura, La Gomera and El Hierro – as well as numerous islets, most of which are uninhabited. Together the Canary Islands cover approximately 7500km² (2895 square miles). They belong geographically to **Macronesia**, a group of

Below: *The Femés valley in the south of the island is noted for its vineyards.*

islands (including Madeira and the Azores) of similar volcanic origin, topography and indigenous flora and fauna. The Canary Islands are about 40 million years old and were formed during the Tertiary geological era (around the same time as the Atlas Mountains in north Africa) as the African tectonic plate moved northeast and created a weakness in the earth's crust through which volcanic material poured. The Canary Islands can best be thought of as the tips of underwater volcanoes. There is also a theory that the two most easterly islands – Lanzarote and Fuerteventura – were once part of the African continent, although there is little proof of this. More evidence suggests that Lanzarote was once connected to Fuerteventura and the islands were separated due to the rise in sea level that followed the Ice Age.

The Volcanic History of Lanzarote

The first volcanic eruptions on Lanzarote occurred between 17 and 20 million years ago and they have continued until recently. Well-documented eruptions took place in the Timanfaya area between 1730 and 1736, when the lava and ash covered around two-thirds of the island and buried many villages and fertile agricultural

Above: *A series of spectacular volcanoes in Timanfaya National Park.*

THE NAME 'CANARY'

There has always been controversy about the origins of the name 'Canary'. There are wild canaries in many parts of the archipelago (although not on Lanzarote), but these birds were probably named after the islands. A popular theory is that early settlers were impressed by the size of the dogs on the islands and used the Latin name for dogs (*canus*) to name the area. A further supposition is that the primitive inhabitants of the islands were Berbers from the Canarii tribe in Morocco.

land in the process. It appears that over 30 volcanoes were spewing out material at this time. A century later, in 1824, there was a further eruption in the same area, but it only lasted for two months. Since then, the volcanoes of Lanzarote have been dormant, but heat remains close to the surface and new eruptions could occur at any time. It is a relief to know that scientists monitor these volcanoes and are able to predict an eruption as long as a week in advance.

Mountains and Rivers

The landscape of Lanzarote has been shaped by its volcanic activity, which has left two main volcanic massifs, Famara-Guatifay in the north and Los Ajaches in the south. Lanzarote's highest mountain, volcano **Peñas del Chache**, rises to 670m (2198ft) and can be seen between the towns of Haría and Los Valles. Further north is **Mount Corona**, rising 609m (1998ft), the eruptions of which led to a huge spread of lava, leaving a wide area of *malpaís* or badlands (the terms apply to a recent lava flow that has not matured sufficiently for a soil to develop for agricultural use). Within the lava are numerous caves or **volcanic tubes**, such as the **Jameos del Agua** and the **Cueva de los Verdes**, which are among the most popular tourist attractions on the island. The massif of Los Ajaches in the south is less dramatic, but it is a fine display of black basalt lava.

The most recent volcanic activity occurred in the southwest of Lanzarote in an area known as **Timanfaya**. This area has been a **national park** since 1974. Nearly three-quarters of the park is covered with lava or ash and is devoid of plant life except for occasional spreads

PLATE TECTONICS AND VOLCANOES

The fairly new science of **Plate Tectonics** has done much in the way of explaining the distribution of the world's volcanoes. Derived from the theory of **Continental Drift**, the science shows that the earth's crust is divided into movable plates. The plate boundaries are lines of weakness through which volcanic magma pours. This explains the series of volcanoes in the mid-Atlantic regions, such as Iceland and the Azores, where the American and European plates are moving apart. The Canary Islands are not on the mid-Atlantic ridge, but lie in an area of weakness. This was caused by the movement that built up the nearby Atlas Mountains in North Africa, as the African plate drifted eastwards.

of lichens. The park has a number of volcanoes over 500m (1650ft) in height, known as the **Montañas del Fuego** (Mountains of Fire), and many other superb volcanic features. Some of the volcanoes have deep craters, such as that on the **Caldera de Corazoncillo**, which is 33m (108ft) deep. In other parts of the park there are small cones, known as *hornitos* (little ovens), formed by exploding gas. The volcanic landscape is extremely colourful, with shades of red, yellow and brown.

Between the volcanic massifs are plains of volcanic ash, gravel and *picón* (small, black, porous volcanic pebbles used in agriculture as a substitute soil), such as **El Rubicón** in the south of the island and **El Jable** in the centre. Surprisingly, these areas are not entirely devoid of fertility, as the *picón* is able to retain sufficient moisture to support vines and other crops.

Lanzarote has no permanently flowing rivers, owing to its low rainfall. There are many *barrancos* (valleys) that have temporary streams during the winter, but the majority of valleys on the island are dry. These *barrancos* were probably formed during the wetter climatic times immediately after the Ice Age.

Seas and Shores

The deep waters of the **Atlantic Ocean** surround Lanzarote and their erosive power has shaped and produced the island's varied coastline. The most spectacular **cliffs**, known as the **Risco de Famara**, are found on the northwest tip of the island. They rise to over 500m (1640ft) and have a number of *miradors* (viewpoints) that provide spectacular views of Isla Graciosa. There are some impressive *puntas* (headlands) where the basalt lava reaches the sea, such

---

THE LEGEND OF ATLANTIS

The legend of the lost continent of Atlantis is a persistent theme in Greek and Roman mythology. The idea was that a large continent, called Atlantis, lay somewhere to the west of Gibraltar. It was thought to be a sort of Utopia, but it had almost entirely slipped under the waves and disappeared. Plato, basing his evidence on the stories of mariners, claimed that only seven mountain tops remained above the waves. Is it a coincidence that the seven main islands of the Canaries all have volcanic peaks?

Opposite: *At El Golfo the sea has eroded into a volcano, flooding its crater and leaving a green-coloured lagoon.*

Below: *The resort of Playa Blanca is backed by a red volcanic cone.*

as Punta Fariones in the north of the island and Punta de Pechiguera – with its prominent lighthouse – in the south. In between the headlands are sandy beaches, some with black volcanic sand and others, like those at **Papagayo**, with golden sand. Some extraordinary features are the result of volcanoes found on the coast itself and a spectacular example is **El Golfo** in the southwest of Lanzarote. Here the sea has breached a volcanic cone and flooded the crater, creating a bright green lagoon, which is a popular tourist attraction.

The coast is also the site of a number of commercial salinas (salt pans), such as **Salinas del Río** in the north and **Salinas de Janubio** in the southwest. The salinas produced salt for the preservation of fish, but today modern cooling plants have replaced this method of salt production. Tourists can still view the salt pans and they provide significant ecological sites on the island as well as important stopovers for migrating birds.

Although the Atlantic Ocean is tidal, the lack of permanent rivers on Lanzarote means that there are no tidal estuaries, except for **Charco de San Ginés** – a sea-water lagoon right at the heart of the island's capital, Arrecife.

There are a few sand dunes on Isla Graciosa and neighbouring Fuerteventura, yet these are not typical features on the coastline of Lanzarote.

Opposite: *The bird of paradise flower, or strelitzia, is common in hotel gardens.*
Right: *Commercial salt pans at Salinas de Janubio in the south of the island.*

Climate

The climate of Lanzarote, along with that of the other Canary Islands, has been described as that of perpetual spring or eternal summer. Unlike the larger islands, such as Tenerife and Gran Canaria, there are no high mountains on Lanzarote, which results in moderate weather patterns on the island. The north of the island, however, is certainly windier than the rest of Lanzarote. The moist **trade winds** blow generally from the north, so that the windward northern coast has a little more rain and cloud than the leeward south, which is somewhat drier and hotter. The differences, however, are not great. The south of the island may enjoy as much as 2500 hours of **sunshine** annually, with temperatures varying from 18° to 24°C (64° to 75°F) in the summer and from 16° to 20°C (61° to 68°F) in the winter, although afternoon temperatures in both winter and summer can be considerably higher. Occasionally during the summer the hot sirocco wind blows from the Sahara bringing desert dust, high temperatures and discomfort to all. Locals refer to this phenomenon as *Tiempo Africano* (African Weather). **Rainfall** is generally light, averaging 117.5mm (4.6in), with the wettest months being January and October. Farmers rely on the nightly fall of dew to aid cultivation. A cool **Canary current** flows from the north and ensures that the sea temperatures around the island are lower than what might be expected at this latitude – being around 18°C (64°F) in the winter and rising to 22°C (72°F) in the summer.

Significantly, the weather makes Lanzarote an ideal all-year-round tourist destination, which is an important factor in the island's economy.

THE BIRD OF PARADISE FLOWER

Although many parts of Lanzarote are barren and infertile, gardens, parks and the environs of hotels are bright with exotic flowers and shrubs that have been brought to the island from many parts of the world. The favourite of most visitors is the **bird of paradise flower** (strelitzia). From glossy dark leaves, flower heads of orange, purple and blue protrude, resembling a crane's head in shape. The flowers make an ideal bedding plant on the island. If you fancy taking a strelitzia home, don't bother to take a cutting, as you can buy them at airport shops, already potted and packed for the journey.

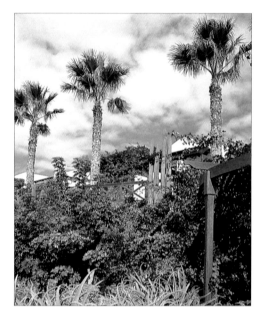

Above: *Palms and bougainvilleas are among the exotic species growing in parks and gardens.*

Flora

The lack of varying altitudes, the recent spread of volcanic material and the arid climate on Lanzarote do not provide an environment for a large range of plant life, such as that on the western islands of the archipelago, to thrive. The plants that are found, however, are of great interest to botanists. Many plants are **indigenous** to the Canary Islands or to a single island. On the lava flows (*malpaís* or badlands), the first plants to grow are mosses (*Bryophyta*) and lichens, while the Canary houseleek (*Aeonuim canariense*) is often the first to appear in cracks and fissures. In more humid parts of the world, the colonization of volcanic material can be rapid, but on arid Lanzarote the process has taken centuries.

Because of its aridity, **trees** are scarce on Lanzarote. A notable exception is in the Haría valley, where hundreds of Canary palms (*Phoenix canariensis*) are found. A few examples of the dragon tree (*Dracaena draco*) may be seen, although these were probably brought from the surrounding islands. The dragon tree, which survives for hundreds of years, is typical of the Canary Islands and was regarded with reverence by the Guanches who were the original inhabitants of the area.

Most of the wild plants seen on Lanzarote are **xerophious**, which means that they have adapted to thrive in dry conditions. Especially common on the scrubland areas are the **spurges** (*euphorbiaceae*) – plants that produce a bitter, milky juice. Growing widely is the candelabra spurge (*Euphorbia canariensis*), which looks like a cactus, and the wild spurge (*Euphorbia*

JOINED TO AFRICA?

A theory suggests that Lanzarote was once joined to Africa. Supporters say that the sand on the island is similar to that of the Sahara, and fossilized eggs of the flightless elephant bird, which was once found on Africa, have been found here. Those who disagree say the sand could have blown over in the sirocco wind, while the eggs might have been brought in by man or be those of a flying bird.

obtusifolia), which has greenish yellow flowers. Near the coast of Lanzarote, the drought-resistant plants are also **halophytic** (salt-tolerant). These plants include seaside plantain (*Plantago aschersonii*), Canary sea lavender (*Limonium tuberculatum*) and sea grape (*Zigophyllum fontanesii*).

Public parks, gardens and the grounds of hotels are bright with **introduced plants**. After the Spanish Conquest, sailors and travellers brought in exotic flowers and shrubs from all over the world. They include bougainvilleas, hibiscuses, geraniums and strelitzias, as well as small trees such as mimosa and jacaranda. All flourish in Lanzarote and many hotel grounds resemble botanical gardens.

Fauna

The amount of animal life on Lanzarote is even less than the variety of flora. With the exception of bats, there is only one indigenous **mammal** on the island, a shrew (*Crocidura canariensis*) which is also found on neighbouring Fuerteventura. There are, however, a number of species that have been introduced to the island, such as the rabbit brought in by the Spaniards in the 14th century, but these are becoming increasingly rare. House mice, hedgehogs and black and brown rats have also settled on the island, and another introduced mammal that almost every visitor will see is the camel. Although they are called *camellos* on the island, they have only one hump and are actually dromedaries. They were introduced from north Africa to assist in agriculture, but are now mainly used to transport tourists around the Timanfaya

Below: *Plants are commonly grown in volcanic pebbles or* picón.

THE USEFUL DRAGON TREE

There are few trees on the island of Lanzarote, but one that is found occasionally is the **dragon tree** (*Dracaena draco*). These trees are believed to live for several centuries, but a precise dating is impossible as they do not produce tree rings. The dragon tree has survived the Ice Age and is a remnant of the Tertiary Geological Era's flora. Traditionally, Guanche meetings took place under a dragon tree. They also used its sap (predictably called dragon's blood, as it turns bright red on exposure to air) to heal wounds, ward off evil spirits and embalm their dead. The sap is also believed to be a cure for leprosy, and for a time it was exported to Italy to stain marble and violins.

National Park. There are numerous **marine mammals** in the waters around Lanzarote and they include several species of whale, porpoise and dolphin. Whale-watching is becoming a popular tourist activity in many parts of the Canary Islands. Monk seals were once bred on Isla de los Lobos, between Lanzarote and Fuerteventura, but they have been hunted to extinction. There are over 400 species of **fish** in the Atlantic around the Canary Islands and the stretch of water between Lanzarote and the African coast is a rich fishing ground, with good catches of *cherne* (stone bass), *sama* (red sea bream), *corvina* (sea bass) and *vieja* (parrot fish) – many of which are on menus at restaurants. Common shellfish include lobsters, prawns and mussels, and there are also game fish such as marlin, tuna, shark and swordfish.

There are few birds in the Canary Islands; only 56 species of birds have been recorded as breeding, and many of these are only spasmodic breeders or in danger of becoming extinct. Lanzarote itself has approximately 30 resident species, so visiting bird-watchers should time their visit to coincide with the spring migration. Of particular interest are the desert species, which include the cream-coloured courser, the Houbara bustard, the trumpeter bullfinch and the Barbary partridge, but they are all difficult to spot. Other common birds are the Berthalot's pipit, the great grey shrike (often seen on telephone wires), the spectacled warbler, the chiffchaff, the linnet, the raven and gulls. Day-trippers to Arrecife should look out for the numerous pairs of cattle egrets that nest in the palm trees on the seafront. Ironically, the wild canary is not found on Lanzarote as it is a woodland bird.

Spring in Lanzarote is a good time to see a beautiful collection of **butterflies**, as many of these colourful creatures spend the summer in Europe, but actually breed in the Canary Islands before migrating. Included in this assortment are the speckled wood, clouded yellow, common blue, cleopatra and migrating monarchs. A moth that is worthy to be mentioned is the silver Y, which is known to migrate north alongside the painted ladies. Common **insects** include the unwelcome mosquito (although not the malaria-carrying type) and dragonflies, including the common red darter.

The **amphibians** and **reptiles** found on the island include lizards, geckoes and skinks. Geckoes are often found in houses and even in hotel bedrooms, where they effectively take care of the insects and are regarded by the locals as a sign of good luck. Thankfully there are no snakes in the Canary Islands! Three species of turtles can be seen in Canarian waters – the leatherback, loggerhead and green. None of them breed here, and they are all threatened species.

HISTORY IN BRIEF

The early history of the Canary Islands is shrouded in myth and mystery. The Greeks and Romans certainly knew of the islands' existence: Plato thought that they were the remains of the lost continent of Atlantis, while the geographer Ptolemy accurately located their position in AD150. It is highly unlikely, however, that either the Greeks nor the Romans ever set foot on the Canary Islands. On the other hand the Phoenicians and the Carthaginians most certainly did.

Above: *The waters around Lanzarote are rich in fish life.*
Opposite: *The raven, distinguished by its croaking call, is Lanzarote's largest bird.*

THE BUTCHER BIRD

One interesting bird among the rather small avian population of Lanzarote is the **great grey shrike** (*Lanius excubitor*) – a handsome black, grey and white bird the size of a blackbird. It spends much of its time on a perch or a telephone wire waving its tail from side to side, searchimg for prey. It can be seen throughout the island, but particularly on farmland, where it catches small birds, mice, lizards and insects. Its habit of impaling its prey on thorns or barbed wire has led to its name – the butcher bird.

Above: *Souvenir shops and restaurants with terraces line the promenade at Playa Blanca.*

Early Inhabitants

Remains of **Cro-Magnon Man** have been found in the Canary Islands. Examples of skulls with broad faces and high foreheads have been carbon dated to around 3000BC. When the Europeans explored the islands in the 14th century, they found a primitive people living there who were tall, blond and blue-eyed. The Tenerife name, the **Guanches**, has been adopted to describe the indigenous people of all the Canary Islands. Nobody is really certain of the origins of the Guanches (although most experts now believe that they were Berbers from North Africa) or how they got to the islands, as they appear to have had no knowledge of boat-building.

Guanche Society

The Europeans explored the islands and found a primitive, Stone-Age community with no knowledge of metals, the wheel, the building of boats or the bow and arrow. The majority lived in caves, which were easily carved out of the soft volcanic ash, although those of higher status lived in simple stone houses that were oval in shape. The Guanche economy was based on animal rearing and the growing of grain crops. The women made pots that were elaborately decorated and used the coil method rather than the wheel. Their clothing was made from sheep- and goatskins, and these animals provided them with meat, cheese and milk. The Guanches also ate fish, fruit and *gofio*, which was a sort of dumpling made from roasted grain flour (*see* panel, page 26).

Despite their primitive way of life, the Guanches had a sophisticated social structure. Their society was divided into castes and they were ruled by an elected king. They worshipped the sun, believed in life after death, and their *faycans* (priests) were regarded as important people. Women played a significant role in society and they could become kings or *faycans*. There was no death penalty, but murderers were severely beaten and their possessions were given to the relatives of their victims as compensation. They also mummified their dead from the highest social strata, using skins and reeds before laying them in burial caves. It is believed that a single Guanche language was spoken (although not written) throughout the islands, with possible local dialects. This suggests that the Guanches had a common origin, since there was very little communication between the various islands.

The Arrival of Europeans

Around 1312, a Genoese navigator named **Lancelotto Malocello** landed on Lanzarote and it is believed that he was responsible for the island's name. He lived on the island for some time before being killed by the Guanches. At this stage the island was familiar to Europeans, and the Portuguese and Spaniards invaded it on numerous occasions and took many of the natives away to be slaves.

The French Connection

A major development in the history of Lanzarote came about in 1402 when two Frenchmen, **Gadifer de la Salle** and **Jean de Béthencourt**, led a small military expedition to Lanzarote. The whole exploit was something of a

---

VERDINO DOGS

It is often claimed that the Canary Islands gained their name from the Latin word *canus*, which means dog. Historical records often mention the large dogs that were found on the islands, and some research suggests that the inhabitants actually ate the dogs. The Spanish Conquistadors were rather scared of these dogs and eventually passed a law to ensure that they be put down, but allowed each shepherd one dog to guard his flocks. Known as **verdinos**, because of the slightly green tinge to their coats, the dogs were smooth-haired with broad jaws. They were noted for their ferocity, but also for their loyalty to their owners. Today there is an organization which aims to keep the verdino strain pure and have it registered as a breed.

Below: *A kid at a farm above Femés. Goats are the most common domestic animals on Lanzarote.*

POLICEMEN

Hopefully, visitors to Lanzarote will not need to contact a policeman – which is just as well, because, confusingly, there are three different Spanish police forces.
Firstly, there are the **Policia Municipal**, who wear blue uniforms and carry out minor duties such as traffic control. There are also the **Policia Nacional**, who have brown uniforms and deal with burglaries and robberies. Finally, there are the **Guardia Civil**, who wear light green uniforms. They were once greatly feared, but now the Guardia Civil have a less important role and spend much of their time on motorcycles doing traffic duty. All Spanish policemen and women are armed and not especially noted for their sense of humour. Don't adopt a frivolous approach towards them!

fiasco as two-thirds of the men deserted in Cádiz, which left around 60 men to land in the north of the island. The Guanche leader, who thought that the French party would protect the islanders from further slave raids, greeted them. De Béthencourt then left for Europe to offer the sovereignty of Lanzarote to whichever court could give him the highest reward. De la Salle, in the meantime, was having trouble with the Guanches and it took a full-scale war before they were finally defeated in 1404. The leader of the Guanches, Guardafía, was baptized along with many of his followers. De Béthencourt, who had been made King of Lanzarote by the Spanish court, returned to the island and succeeded de la Salle. He then recruited a number of *Lanzaroteños* and set out to conquer the rest of the Canary Islands. He swiftly overcame Fuerteventura, el Hierro and La Gomera, and left his nephew, Maciot, in charge while returning to France. Maciot married the daughter of the Guanche leader and set up his headquarters at Teguise. Within the next few years the first churches were built on the island.

The Spanish Conquest

The capture of Lanzarote, Fuerteventura and La Gomera was, in fact, no great feat, because the small Guanche population on these islands had been decimated by diseases that were introduced by the Europeans during the years of slave trading. The larger and more populated islands of Gran Canaria and Tenerife rendered a more determined resistance.

Below: *The roads of Lanzarote are patrolled by police motorcyclists.*

Spain began the second phase of the Conquest in 1478, when Ferdinand and Isabella, *Los Reyes Católicos* (the Catholic monarchs), sanctioned an attack on Gran Canaria. The Spanish forces met fierce resistance from the Guanches and the turning point came when a new military

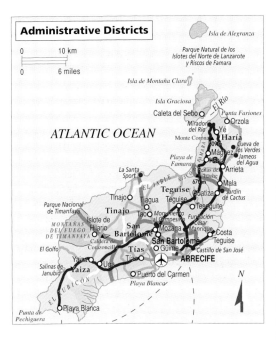

Administrative Districts

Isla de Alegranza

0   10 km
0   6 miles

Parque Natural de los
Islotes del Norte de Lanzarote
y Riscos de Famara

Isla de Montaña Clara

ATLANTIC OCEAN

Isla Graciosa

Caleta del Sebo   Punta Fariones
          Mirador   Orzola
          del Río   Yé
Monte Corona   Haria
                              Cueva de
                              los Verdes
Playa de   Máguez   Jameos
Famara   del Agua
La Santa   Arrieta
Sport
                          670m   Mala
      Teguise   Guatiza   Jardin
Tinajo   Tiagua Teguise   de Cactus
Tinajo   Tao   Teseguite
Parque Nacional   Monumento
de Timanfaya   al Campesino César
MONTAÑAS   Hilario San   Manrique
DEL FUEGO   Bartolomé Mozaga   Costa
DE TIMANFAYA   Teguise
El Golfo   Caldera de   Güime   Castillo de San José
      Corazoncillo Tías
      Yaiza   Tías   ARRECIFE
Salinas de Yaiza Uga   N
Janubio   Puerto del Carmen
                  Playa Blanca
Punta de   Playa Blanca
Pechiguera

governor, **Pedro de Vera**, arrived in 1480. He applied aggressive tactics and eventually persuaded the two local Guanche kings to convert to Christianity. Nevertheless, it was 1483 before Gran Canaria was completely defeated.

The next Spanish commander on the scene was **Alonso Fernández de Lugo**, who in 1491 received royal assent to attack La Palma and Tenerife. La Palma was quickly taken, but Tenerife was to prove the toughest island to overcome. De Lugo arrived on the island in 1493 with a force of 1000 soldiers plus Guanche mercenaries from other islands. There were a number of battles and de Lugo had to send for extra men from Spain before Tenerife was finally overcome.

Post-Conquest Guanches

After the Conquest, the various islands were administered for Spain by *capitanes-generales*. Many Guanches

Above: *Vines growing in volcanic gravel sheltered by stone walls.*

died from European diseases to which they had no resistance, and a large number of them were taken to Spain as slaves (although many were allowed to return). Others assumed Spanish names and were converted to Christianity. Assimilation with the colonists came swiftly and the Guanches' spoken language quickly disappeared. Despite this, modern anthropological research claims that several of Guanche characteristics are evident in the everyday life on the Canary Islands. Certainly a great number of the inhabitants of the Canary Islands are very proud of their Guanche ancestry, as they feel that this highlights the difference between themselves and mainland Spaniards.

Spanish Colonial Rule

For the next three or four centuries the Canary Islands experienced mixed fortunes under Spanish colonial rule. The islands attracted large numbers of settlers, not only from Spain, but also from Portugal, France and Italy. After Columbus's discovery of the New World in 1492, ports such as Las Palmas on Gran Canaria and Santa Cruz on Tenerife became important staging posts for ships travelling to and from the Americas. Lanzarote, with no suitable harbour, gained little from this trans-atlantic business. Since Lanzarote is the most easterly island in the archipelago, it also attracted more than its fair share of corsairs from countries opposed to Spain, such as Britain, Holland and Portugal, while pirates from the north coast of Africa were always a threat, sacking Teguise on numerous occasions.

Consequently, a number of fortresses were built, including Santa Bárbara near Teguise, the Castillo de San Gabriel to protect Arrecife, and the Tower of San Marcial del Rubicón in the south of the island. By the 19th century, invasions by buccaneers had become less of a problem and this allowed the island's capital to move from Teguise to the port of Arrecife in 1852.

Boom and Bust

During the years of Spanish colonial rule, the Canary Islands experienced turbulent economic fortunes. Reliance on various types of monoculture led to cycles of 'boom and bust' and mass emigrations to the New World. The first industry to collapse was that of **sugar cane**, due to the abolition of slavery and the cheaper sugar produced in central and southern America. Lanzarote was fortunate as it was never able to specialize in sugar cane because of its dry climate. Sugar was replaced by the production of **wine**. The wine boom, however, was over by the start of the 19th century, because of the competition from Madeira and diseases affecting the vines. This led to further emigration.

In 1825, a new product was discovered. This was **cochineal** (a red dye), which was extracted from a small parasitic insect found on cactus plants. Thousands of prickly pear cactus plants soon appeared on Lanzarote and this unusual type of farming boomed. By the 1870s chemical dyes began to appear on the market and the cochineal trade fell away, which resulted in yet more emigration. Strangely though, both wine and cochineal continue to be produced on Lanzarote, more so than on any of the other Canary Islands.

> **MORE AFRICAN THAN SPANISH**
>
> One usually associates **bullfighting**, **flamenco** and **paella** with Spain, although none of these associations are typically Canarian. Most *Lanzaroteños* would regard bullfighting as barbaric, and anything resembling a bull-ring in Lanzarote is probably a wrestling arena. Flamenco is essentially Andalucían gypsy music, and *Canarios* have closer links with Latin American music. Genuine paella originated in the Valencia area and was basically a meat and rice dish. *Lanzaroteños*, however, produce a seafood version to satisfy the tourists. Many people in the Canary Islands actively reject these mainland traditions and prefer to stress their African links.

Below: *Prickly pear. This succulent is a host plant for the cochineal beetle.*

PETROL IN LANZAROTE

Most hire cars in Lanzarote take unleaded petrol, which is known in Spanish as *sin plomo*. There are plenty of petrol stations on the island and their positions are shown on all the road maps that are on sale. The maps show, however, that there are no petrol stations on the road through La Geria or to the north of Arrieta. Most stations accept credit cards and many still have attendant service. Tourists will be pleased to find that petrol in Lanzarote is cheaper than in the UK and in many other countries.

Below: *Erosion of soft volcanic pumice has produced some fantastic rock outcrops in many parts of the island.*

Political Developments

The Canary Islands were declared a province of Spain in 1821, with Santa Cruz de Tenerife as the capital. Rivalry between Tenerife and Gran Canaria was prevalent, with Tenerife proving to dominate, while Lanzarote – with its small population and lack of economic clout – gradually became something of a political backwater.

A measure of political independence was established in 1912 when Spain introduced island councils or *cabildos*. In 1927 the Spanish government divided the Canary Islands into two provinces. The Eastern Province included Lanzarote, Fuerteventura and Gran Canaria, with its capital at Las Palmas, while the Western Province was made up of Tenerife and the smaller islands of La Gomera, El Hierro and La Palma, with the capital at Santa Cruz de Tenerife.

The Canary Islands' economy showed an upturn during the late 19th and early 20th centuries. This was influenced by their designation as a **free trade zone** and the growth of the Atlantic steamship trade. In the 1850s, British entrepreneurs introduced banana and tomato farming to the islands, but unfortunately Lanzarote's arid climate was unsuitable for these crops. The disruption caused by two world wars led to unemployment and a further wave of emigration to the Americas. The extent of this emigration is illustrated by the fact that over a quarter of a million people of Canary Island origin are estimated to live in Caracas, the capital of Venezuela. The full story of the history of emigration can be seen in the Museum of the Emigrant in Castillo de Santa Bárbara, just outside the old capital of Teguise. In the 19th century, Lanzarote's population was reduced by over a third, but it stabilized during the 20th century after the discovery of the *enarenado* system of agriculture, which uses volcanic clinker to preserve water.

The Rise of Franco

In the 1930s the Canary Islands found themselves to be involved in the Spanish Civil War. In March 1936, General Franco, who was suspected of planning a coup to overthrow the government, was exiled to Tenerife with the post of *Comandante-General*. Franco was in the Canary Islands

Above: *The regional flag of the Canary Islands is flown on all public occasions.*

HISTORICAL CALENDAR

3000BC Archaeological evidence from skulls suggests that the Canary Islands were inhabited by Cro-Magnon Man.

1100BC Phoenicians and Carthaginians are believed to have visited the Canary Islands.

1312 Genoese explorer, Lancelotto Malocello, occupies and names Lanzarote.

1340 Portugal and Spain send ships to investigate the islands, finding Guanches living a Stone-Age existence.

1401 Spanish Conquest begins with an expedition led by Jean de Béthencourt, who soon conquers Lanzarote. He makes a treaty with the local Guanche king who welcomes protection from pirate raids. Lanzarote becomes a base for attacks on the other islands, using a number of Guanche mercenaries.

1483 Gran Canaria is finally subdued.

1492 Columbus makes his first visit to the Canary Islands and observes an eruption of Mount Teide on Tenerife.

1494 Tenerife is the last island to fall to the Spanish forces.

15th and 16th centuries The Spanish colonize the islands, with the settlers developing a thriving economy, aided by the slave trade. Navies and buccaneers of rival countries pose a constant threat. Lanzarote, because of its exposed position, is often attacked by pirates from North Africa, who take inhabitants away as slaves.

1730–36 Volcanic eruptions on Lanzarote destroy many villages and large areas of farmland, leading to mass emigration to Latin America.

Early 18th century The cochineal industry reaches its peak on Lanzarote.

1852 Isabella II declares the Canaries a Free Trade Zone.

1927 Canaries divided into two zones, with Las Palmas as capital of the Eastern Province, consisting of Gran Canaria, Lanzarote and Fuerteventura.

1936 General Franco plots a military coup, leading to the Spanish Civil War. Lanzarote is affected by the closure of the trade routes.

1970s Tourism begins to take off in Lanzarote.

1982 Regional Constitution granted by Spain to the Canary Islands.

1986 Canary Islands granted special status within the European Union.

2002 Introduction of the Euro.

Above: *The attractive town hall in San Bartolomé in central Lanzarote.*

for a mere four months, but during this time he survived three assassination attempts. He eventually went to Morocco to lead the insurgents, and began the brutal Civil War that was to divide towns and families throughout Spain.

The Growth of Tourism

Franco largely ignored the Canary Islands while he was in power in Spain, giving rise to an active separatist movement in the archipelago. The movement was only stemmed in 1982, when the Canaries (and other parts of Spain) were given autonomous powers and a regional constitution. Another factor that quelled nationalism was the growth of **tourism**, which has provided considerable employment and is now Lanzarote's main source of convertible revenue. Indeed the number of tourists on the island often exceeds the number of indigenous inhabitants.

GOVERNMENT AND ECONOMY
Government

The two provinces of the Canary Islands form one of the 17 autonomous regional communities in Spain. Rivalry between the islands is part of their history and the regional government has offices in both Santa Cruz de Tenerife and Las Palmas on Gran Canaria. The regional government has powers covering transport, agriculture, health and policing, and it also has the ability to raise local taxes. Each island has its own local administration known as the *cabildo*, while a further level of adminstration is the district or *municipio*. Lanzarote is divided into seven administrative districts – Haría, Teguise, Arrecife, Tinajo, San Bartolomé, Tías and Yaiza (see map, page 19) – so that burgeoning holiday resorts can be administered conveniently.

THE RABBIT HUNTERS

It is a common habit in Spain to give the inhabitants of towns or regions certain names that are related to their past way of life. The people of Lanzarote, for example, are known as **conejeros**, which is translated as rabbit hunters. But where are these rabbits on the island? Few visitors will ever see these animals in the wild (there are very few to be hunted for food) and if rabbit is offered on a restaurant's menu, it will probably have been reared domestically. It is possible, of course, that rabbits once thrived on Lanzarote and were wiped out by the 18th-century volcanic eruptions.

The main **political parties** are the left-wing Partido Socialista Obrero Español (PSOE) and the right-of-centre Partido Popular (PP). In the 1990s various nationalist groups merged to form the Coalición Canaria (CC), which now – rather than pressing for independence – pushes Madrid for improvements. Most recent governments have been coalitions between the various parties.

The Economy

Canarian **agriculture** has diversified over the years, as farmers have learnt that farming a single product is not profitable in the long run, and now most farms have a variety of enterprises. The number of crops that can be grown on Lanzarote is somewhat restricted by the dry climate and lack of irrigation, especially in comparison to the larger and more mountainous islands to the west. Onions, tomatoes and potatoes are the major crops and all of these are grown in abundance. Wine from the *malvasía* grape is exported, mainly to the other Canary Islands. Other crops include various types of legumes, melons and tobacco. The basis of all crop farming on Lanzarote is the *enarenado* method, whereby plants are grown in black volcanic gravel or *picón*, which has the ability to absorb dew and prevent evaporation. Livestock is rare on Lanzarote and visitors to the island are unlikely to see any cattle or sheep. Goats and donkeys are kept and the occasional camel is still seen working in the fields.

The other traditional mainstay of the Lanzarote economy is **fishing**. There are rich fishing grounds between the east of the island and the African coast, and Arrecife is the second-largest fishing port in the Canary Islands. Large numbers of sardines, sea bass, *vieja* and cod are caught here. Associated

> **GOATS' CHEESE**
>
> Although there are no cattle kept on Lanzarote (as there is no grass to feed them), there are over 8000 goats. Formerly farmed for their milk, they are now largely used for cheese production. The cheese varies in appearance – it can be yellow and hard or white and crumbly. Generally speaking, the darker the colour, the better it keeps. One interesting variety is called *ahumado*, which is smoked over prickly pear leaves. Lanzarote goats' cheese is on sale in all supermarkets, and all self-catering visitors should certainly try some.

Below: *Tomato cultivation invariably takes place on the black volcanic soil.*

GOFIO

This is one of the few culinary items to have survived since Guanche times. *Gofio* was once made from the glasswort plant, but after the Spanish introduced Indian maize, this became the main ingredient. It is mixed with wheat flour and toasted (or roasted). It is then used in a variety of ways: it can be sprinkled on food, used to thicken stews or soups, made into a breakfast food, or mixed with figs or almonds to make a dessert. Unfortunately, few visitors to Lanzarote get the opportunity to try *gofio*, as it is rarely on the menu in the main tourist resorts. Those who are keen to try this Canarian food need to drive into the interior of the island in order to find a rural restaurant that has *gofio* on the menu.

industries include canning and the production of fish bone meal. Vast numbers of fish can be seen in the clear waters of Lanzarote's harbours, and a popular habit of tourists is to throw bread to the fish – the waters seem to boil with fish desperate for a bite.

In recent years there has been a startling growth in **tourism**. The Canary Islands are an all-year-round destination attracting over 8½ million (1998) visitors annually, mainly from Britain, Germany, Scandinavia, Holland and mainland Spain. Of this total, Lanzarote attracts around 1½ million tourists annually. Tourism also provides a vast number of jobs in the construction industry, which has been booming over the last decade. It is estimated that over 90 per cent of the working population of Lanzarote is involved with tourism in some way. The income from tourism has had the effect of improving the island's infrastructure to the benefit of *Lanzaroteños* and visitors alike. Nevertheless, 16 per cent of the population is unemployed (although there is a sizeable grey economy, which according to statistics represents the unemployed, as they do not declare their earnings on tax returns) and average wages are among the lowest in the EU.

THE PEOPLE

The total **population** of the Canary Islands currently stands at 1,610,000 and grows at a rate of more than 1 per cent annually. The last census found that Lanzarote has 80,000 inhabitants, half of whom live in the capital, Arrecife. These totals include a good number of foreign residents, mainly from Britain and Germany. There are also small numbers from Latin America, largely made up of returning emigrants from such countries as Cuba and Venezuela. The people of Lanzarote are mainly descendants of Spaniards and they are generally dark haired and have an olive complexion. They are fiercely patriotic and regard themselves as *Canarios*, rather than from the 'peninsula', which is their name for mainland Spain. They have mixed feelings towards mainland Spaniards, call them *godos* (or Goths) and accuse them of taking local jobs. Indeed, many *Canarios* like to think of themselves as African rather than Spanish. Employers, however, often prefer to offer jobs to the mainland Spaniards, whom they regard as more reliable.

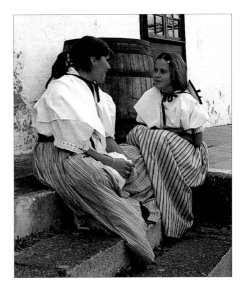

Like mainland Spaniards, *Canarios* are family-orientated. Machismo is still prevalent, but women have become increasingly liberated and now play a large role in public life, with many employed in the tourist industry.

Above: *Women in local costume at a* feria *at Teguise.*
Opposite: *Gutted fish hang on a line to dry in the fishing port of Orzola.*

Religion

The Spanish invaders brought **Roman Catholicism** with them to the Canary Islands and they swiftly converted the Guanches. It is still the official religion and it plays an important part in the lives of the people. Although weekly church attendance is not very high, most *Canarios* have church baptisms, weddings and funerals and attend church for various religious events noted on their calendar.

Festivals

Fiestas are the traditional way of celebrating Saints' days on the religious calendar. These include Easter (*Semana Santa*); *Corpus Christi*, when floral carpets are laid out on

---

CHILD-FRIENDLY ISLAND

Do not worry about taking babies or young children to Lanzarote, as they are made very welcome. Local children keep very late nights and are not excluded from any family activities. Waiters traditionally make a huge fuss of small children who come to their restaurants and prepare special portions for them. Older children will find plenty to occupy themselves, from sandy beaches to theme parks and boat trips.

Above: *The simple lines of the whitewashed church at Playa Blanca.*

the streets; and the Fiestas del Carmen, marked by processions of boats. *Romerías* are processions led by decorated ox carts, which head from town churches to a hermitage (a place where a revered image is kept) or similar location. There are many festivals of a secular nature and these may include a week-long *feria* (fair). Fiestas on Lanzarote are usually accompanied by fireworks, bonfires, parades, wrestling matches and traditional folk dancing and singing.

Sport and Recreation

The Canary Islands have some unique forms of sports that go back centuries and are enthusiastically followed by the locals. *Lucha Canaria* (Canarian wrestling) had its origins in Guanche trials of strength. Bullfighting is not popular in the Canary Islands, but sand-covered arenas resembling bullrings are used for wrestling competitions. Each village has its own wrestling team and *luchas* (competitions) are often held at original Guanche locations during fiestas. *Juego del Palo* (stick fighting) also originated in pre-Conquest days. It is a contest using 2m (6.6ft) wooden staves called *banot* with which contestants aim to do maximum damage to each other. Even longer staves of around 2.5m (8.2ft) are used in the *Salto del Regaton de la Garrocha*, a form of pole vaulting in which contestants leap down a mountainside and across deep ravines. Less appealing to tourists is **cock fighting**, which has a strong following in Lanzarote.

The more international spectator sports are also extremely popular in the Canary Islands. As in the rest of Spain, **football** is obsessively followed. UD Las

---

THE CEREMONY OF THE DYING SARDINE

Many of the coastal fiestas in the Canary Islands end with a curious ceremony involving a giant mock-up of a sardine. It is often 'rescued' from the beach and taken to a shopping centre by an entourage of doctors and nurses. An emergency operation is carried out in an 'operating theatre', but the sardine always dies. There is a funeral procession through the streets and its last will and testament is read out by a famous personality. The giant sardine is finally cremated on a huge bonfire. The fireworks then begin and this marks the end of the fiesta.

Palmas are in the Spanish second division and their
local matches against rival Club Deportivo Tenerife are
among the highlights of the Canary Islands' sporting
year. There are plenty of activities available for visitors
to Lanzarote and it is possible to base a holiday around
sport by staying at **Club la Santa** near Tinajo, in the
northwest of the island, and rub shoulders with world-
famous sportsmen and women. Lanzarote's only **golf**
course is at Costa Teguise, and most of the large hotels
offer **tennis** and **swimming** facilities. The Atlantic
Ocean offers many possibilities for **water sports**, for
locals and tourists alike. **Surfing** (particularly on the
north coast), **sailing**, **windsurfing** and **power-boat
racing** are all highly popular. The clear and warm
waters of the Atlantic are perfect for **scuba diving** and
snorkelling, and there are a number of undersea natural
parks around the shores of the islands. The ocean also
provides ideal conditions for **game fishing**. Charter
boats are available for swordfish, tuna, shark and
marlin fishing. Other recreational activities on offer in
Lanzarote include **cycling** (bikes can be hired at most
resorts), **horse riding** (there are a number of equestrian
centres where horses may be hired) and **karting**.

LANZAROTE'S CHURCHES

Although there are no
cathedrals on Lanzarote,
there is an interesting
selection of churches to visit.
Many churches date from the
early 16th century and display a variety of styles. Few
are genuinely **Gothic** as this
style was on the way out
when the Spaniards were
colonizing the islands, but
there are many examples of
the **Mudéjar** style, which
had its origins in the Moorish
occupation of southern
Spain. Other churches display
the ornate **Plateresque** decoration named after the work
of silversmiths. Look out for
some marvellously carved
wooden ceilings. Stained-
glass windows are generally
uninspiring, but this is more
than compensated for by the
superb decorating of
interiors. The altar screens
(*retablos*) are often
elaborately carved and dripping with gold leaf. Many
churches have carvings by
Luján Pérez (1756–1815),
the greatest of Canarian
sculptors. When visiting
Lanzarote's churches,
remember that beachwear is
inappropriate and not
appreciated by the locals.

Left: *Sailboarding at Costa
Teguise; this has become
one of Lanzarote's fastest
growing sports.*

SPANISH-STYLE SNACKS

Tapas are believed to have originated in Sevilla during the 19th century, when drinkers protected their glasses of *fino* from dust, flies and dripping hams by putting a *tapa* (cover) over their glass. The cover was often a slice of bread on which enterprising bartenders began to add food. The rest, as they say, is history. Spain's quirky meal times encourage taking the occasional snack to fill the gap. The days when a free *tapa* was provided with a drink are largely over, but a *tapas* crawl is one of the delights that the Canary Islands have to offer. *Tapas* vary from a simple dish of olives, or a slice of cheese, to quite sophisticated dishes. Remember, it is cheaper to take your *tapas* standing at a bar than sitting at a table.

Food and Drink

The **food** of Lanzarote illustrates a wide range of influences from other countries, including mainland Spain, northern Europe and even the Americas. Typical Canarian food is most likely to be found in the capital, Arrecife, and the inland towns and villages, rather than in the main resorts, where restaurants tend to serve international food with a Spanish flavour. If the visitor wishes to sample true Canarian food then the unusual meal times must be appreciated. **Breakfast** (*desayuno*) is generally light and rarely served before 09:30. It usually consists of coffee, a sandwich (*bocadillo*) or a small cake (*pastel*). **Lunch** (*almuerzo*) is usually eaten after 14:30 and may have been preceded by *tapas*, which are light snacks served at the bar. Lunch, for many *Canarios*, is the main meal of the day and dinner (*cena*) is a lighter meal, which is usually eaten after 22:00.

There are two fares in Lanzarote that the visitor should certainly sample. One is *gofio* (ground and toasted wheat or maize), the island's traditional staple food, which goes back to Guanche times. The other is *papas arrugadas*, small new potatoes with wrinkly skins, which are boiled in very salty water and served with most main courses.

Main meals in the resort restaurants of Lanzarote are usually introduced with a starter, such as a salad (*ensalada*) or a soup (*sopa*). Particular favourites are fish soup (*sopa de pescada*) and vegetable soup (*sopa de verdura*). Most restaurants also offer the popular mainland cold soup, *gazpacho*, which consists of finely chopped onions, tomatoes and garlic. The main course usually includes meat (*carne*) or fish (*pescado*). The most commonly offered meats are beef (*ternera*), chicken (*pollo*), lamb (*cordero*), pork (*cerdo*)

Left: *Canarian lunch – lentil soup, Canarian fish, sauces and potatoes.*
Opposite: *Cooked mussels* (mejiones) *with herbs is a typical Canarian dish.*

and rabbit (*conejo*). The prolific wild rabbits are hunted on the island or reared domestically for the table, but the other meat is imported. The meat may be grilled (*a la parilla*), roasted (*asado*) or it may be prepared in a stew (*estafado* or *puchero*).

A mouth watering variety of **fish** and **shellfish** are also found on menus, with some significant differences to the selection found on Spain's Mediterranean coast. Fish is usually prepared simply, being fried (*frito*) or grilled (*a la plancha*). At some of the better fish restaurants, it is possible to choose your own fish from a tank or a display refrigerator, but the price is subject to the weight of the fish. The most common fish on the menu are sea bass (*cherne*), hake (*merluza*), swordfish (*pez espada*), sole (*lenguado*), tuna (*atun* or *bonito*) and parrotfish (*vieja*). Some excellent shellfish is also available, including prawns (*gambas*), mussels (*mejiones*) and squid (*calamares*). Particular Canarian specialities are the sauces that are provided with both the fish and meat dishes. The red *mojo rojo* is a spicy vinaigrette-type sauce made from a mixture of chilli, cumin, paprika and saffron, and usually served with meat. *Mojo verde* is a green variation prepared with coriander or parsley instead of paprika, making a perfect accompaniment to fish. Vegetables are rather limited on Lanzarote and salad is usually

THE UNUSUAL *TIMPLE*

On the island of Lanzarote, most traditional dancing and songs are accompanied by the *timple* (pronounced tim-play). It is a stringed instrument, similar to the ukulele and the mandolin, made of wood and it has a rounded back. It normally has five strings, although there is a four-stringed version called the *contra* that is found on Lanzarote, but not on any of the other islands. Once thought to have originated from the Spanish *guitarillo*, it is now believed to have been brought to the islands by Berber slaves. The *timple* is played at local fiestas. It was even exported to Latin American countries with the many waves of emigrants, and it characterizes the folk music of both Cuba and Venezuela. On Lanzarote, the *timple* is traditionally made in the old capital of Teguise. The souvenir shops at Lanzarote airport sell CDs featuring *timple* music, and the instruments themselves are a fitting souvenir of a holiday on the island.

Above: *A chef descales fish for his restaurant on the beach at Playa Blanca.*

CHURROS

Breakfast for most working *Lanzaroteños* is a hurried affair, often taken in a bar en route to work, rather than at home. Coffee and toast or a pastry probably satisfies most people, but the islanders have a sweet tooth and there are many devotees of **churros**. These are short sticks of a sort of deep-fried doughnut, which are dipped in a drink of hot chocolate. They are very fattening!

served as a garnish to most main dishes.

The choice of **desserts** (*postres*) is usually confined to traditional Spanish favourites such as crème caramel (*flan*), ice cream (*helado*) or fruit (*fruta*). You might be lucky enough to be offered a traditional local dessert such as *frangollas* (a corn-based milk pudding flavoured with cinnamon, honey and brandy) or *torrijas* (sweet fritters of maize flour flavoured with honey and aniseed). Bananas are grown on neighbouring islands and they are a favourite dessert. They are often served fried with a topping of sugar, brandy and lemon juice. Any local cheese on offer will be goat's milk cheese, or *queso blanca* (*see* panel, page 25), which is produced near Teguise.

The main resort areas in the south of Lanzarote also offer a bewildering variety of foreign restaurants. Chinese restaurants are particularly common, but many other nationalities are also represented. English breakfasts are offered in many places. Visitors on a budget should try the menu of the day (*menu del día*), which usually includes a starter, main course and a dessert, as well as bread and a drink, for a bargain price.

Sampling local **alcoholic drinks** is a pleasant part of many people's holiday, and Lanzarote offers plenty of choices at very reasonable prices. You will find **wine** from many parts of the world in the local supermarkets, but one must try the local *malvasía* wine, which is cultivated in the La Geria, San Bartolomé and Mozaga areas. Look particularly for the award-winning *El Grifo* wine – but beware, the *malvasías* can be 17 per cent proof and similar to a sherry in strength. Most wines served in restaurants, however, are from the Spanish mainland. There are some popular wine-based summer drinks, including *tinto de verano*, a mixture of red wine and lemonade, and the deceptively strong *sangria*, which is a combination of red wine, lemonade and liqueurs, garnished with fruit and ice. The most common **beers** are *Dorada*, which is made on Tenerife, and *Tropical* from Gran Canaria. There are also beers from the Spanish mainland, such as *San Miguel* and *Cruz Campo*, as well as a host of foreign brews. For a small draught beer ask for *una caña*. The best-known Canarian spirit is rum (*ron*), which is made from locally grown sugar cane on Gran Canaria. The same factory also makes *ron miel*, a rum liqueur with added honey. There are a number of other **liqueurs** made from the subtropical fruits grown on the larger, wetter islands of the archipelago. The most popular is *cobana*, a yellow banana liqueur that comes in a striking bottle. Remember that spirit measures (if they are used at all) are two or three times larger than one would expect at home.

The most popular **non-alcoholic** drink is coffee, which comes in a variety of forms. Any bar with a good reputation will make its coffee in an espresso machine; for an espresso-type coffee, ask either for a *café solo* (which is black) or *café cortado* (which has just a drop of milk). *Café con leche* is milky coffee. Don't be surprised if your coffee arrives in a glass. *Canarios* often take a shot of rum in their coffee or have an accompanying *coñac*.

Tea is also available, but usually served rather weak. A chocolate drink with breakfast is popular among *Lanzaroteños*, who often dunk their *churros* (a form of doughnut) into the beverage. A full range of soft drinks (*refrescos*) and fruit juices (*zumos*) are also available.

NIGHTLIFE

Compared with Tenerife and Gran Canaria, nightlife on Lanzarote is relatively subdued. This is definitely not 'lager lout' territory. Most entertainment takes place in the **Centros Comerciales**. Shopping centres by day, their bars and discos start livening up in the late evening and some may stay open for most of the night. Older revellers may find that the **Casino de Lanzarote** at Puerto del Carmen has some attractions. The gambling hall is open from 20:00 until 04:00. Gamblers have to be over 18 and an ID may be required to enter.

Below: *Tasting wine at El Grifo Wine Museum near Masdache.*

Above: *Sculpted fallen angels at Teguise market.*
Opposite: *One of the many wind sculptures and mobiles found in public places. They were designed by César Manrique.*

Crafts

Tourists find a wide variety of crafts to take home as souvenirs. The production of craft articles is a major source of income for many of the rural villages of Lanzarote. Sadly, however, many of the items on sale in souvenir shops are cheap imitations from abroad, and this is a considerable threat to the survival of ancient craft skills on the island. Many of the handicrafts that are so admired by tourists were once essential to the daily agricultural way of life in past centuries.

Fine **woodwork** can be seen in the ornately carved balconies in the older towns and villages of Lanzarote, and on furniture, chests and carved figures. The making of *timples*, a traditional Canarian stringed instrument (*see* panel, page 31), is centred on Teguise. **Basketwork**, using wood, cane, straw, as well as palm and banana leaves, is a common craft throughout the island. Examples include fans, baskets and bags, while the finely woven straw hats from Yaiza and Tinajo make excellent souvenirs. The craft of pottery has its beginnings in Guanche times and it is still made in the traditional way – without using a wheel. The pots vary in size – from large urns that were used to store olive oil down to small vases and ashtrays. Look out for the tiny *Idolos de Tara* (Guanche-style figurines) and for the *pinterderas* (clay seals with an imprint or design) which were probably used as brooches. It is possible to visit the studios of some of Lanzarote's potteries and watch these skilled artisans at work. Probably the most attractive souvenirs (and the lightest to carry home) are the **textiles**. Exquisitely embroidered cloth is seen in the colourful national costumes that are worn at local festivals. Tablecloths, napkins and handkerchiefs are the most commonly displayed items, but these are also the craft goods that are

FLOWER CARPETS

It is a common practice in Spain to make flower-petal patterns on the pavements for the **Corpus Christi** religious festival in late May or early June. In the Canary Islands it has become a fine art, with the designs being either geometric, floral or depicting scenes from the Bible. In Tenerife, coloured volcanic soil is used for the decoration, while in Gran Canaria they mainly stick to flowers. In Lanzarote, on the other hand, they use dyed salt for the patterns, reflecting their long tradition of salt production. Ironically, so little salt is produced on the island today that most of the material for the 'flower' carpets has to be imported!

most often brought in from abroad. Look for the genuine articles at artisan shops. Other interesting craft souvenirs include rag dolls in national costume, lacework made by the island's nuns, and jewellery fashioned from olivine – a dark green semi-precious volcanic mineral. One of the best ways to find gifts is to visit one of the island's flea markets. The most popular is the Sunday morning market at Teguise, which attracts coach loads of tourists from all over the island. You will find, however, that goods made by foreigners living on Lanzarote far out-number the local craft items sold here. Other possibilities are the Pueblo Marinero centre at Costa Teguise on Friday evenings, and the Punta Limones centre at Playa Blanca on Wednesday mornings.

The Arts

Although the Guanches left numerous examples of wall paintings in caves, it took some time before any notable Canary Island **painters** emerged. Most of the 17th-, 18th- and 19th-century artists confined their work to religious themes and some of their paintings may be seen in churches on the island. One of the best-known artists was Néstor de la Torre (1887–1938), who spe-cialized in murals and was responsible for a campaign to revive Canarian folk art and architecture. The work of the versatile César Manrique – artist, sculptor, architect and environmentalist – can be seen throughout the Canary Islands and particu-larly in his native Lanzarote.

José Luján Pérez (1756–1815) is a renowned **sculptor** and his work can be seen in churches and cathedrals throughout the Canary Islands. Although the Guanches had no written language, **literature** has a long history in the Canary Islands. Indeed there is a well-known saying that 'the Canary Islands is a land of poets'. There have been many novelists and poets over

CANARIAN WRESTLING

Lucha Canaria or Canarian wrestling has strict rules. There are two teams of 12 participants or *luchadores*. Two contestants at a time attempt to throw each other to the ground in the best of three competitions or *brega*. Only the soles of the feet must touch the ground. Canarian wrestling is not a violent sport, as punching and kicking are not allowed. Skill and balance are more important than weight and size. The team that wins the most *bregas* claims the over-all match. The villages of Uga and Los Valles are particularly noted for their *luchadores*.

the centuries, but most of them have had to move to the mainland to gain recognition for their work. Perhaps the best-known novelist was Benito Pérez Galdós (1843–1920) who hailed from Las Palmas, Gran Canaria.

There are some fine **museums and art galleries** in the Canary Islands, although Lanzarote is lacking in this respect. Undoubtedly the best art gallery to visit is the **International Museum of Contemporary Art** located in the 18th-century Castillo de San José overlooking the harbour in Arrecife. It has an excellent permanent collection and special exhibitions.

Music and Dance

Although the Canary Islands have not produced any well-known composers, classical music is taken seriously and concerts are always well supported. Traditional folk music and dancing are usually observed at fiestas. Dances include the lively *isa* and the more dignified *folia*. Occasionally the *tajaraste*, a dance believed to have its origins in Guanche times, may be performed. Traditional instruments, such as the *characas* (castanets) and the *timple* (which is like a five-stringed ukelele), accompany the dancing. Immigrants from Andalucía have introduced many dances, such as the *malagueña* and the *sevillaña*. The village of San Bartolomé is particularly famed for its folk music. Other popular music includes Latin American *salsa* rhythms.

Architecture

The Guanches, who were largely cave-dwellers, left little legacy in the way of vernacular architecture. The oldest buildings in Lanzarote date back to the Spanish Conquest. Over several centuries, raids by Barbary pirates and buccaneers from Spain's nautical rivals reduced many of the older buildings to ruins. Nevertheless, some of Lanzarote's ancient houses are in a good state of preservation. The Gothic style was on its way out at the time of the Conquest and many of the early buildings, especially churches, were constructed in the *Mudéjar* style, which had been bequeathed to the Spaniards by the Moors. In domestic design, the *Mudéjar* style encompasses the need for water and protection from the sun. Most houses are built around a central courtyard or *patio*, often with a decorated well. In the larger houses, the *patio* has shady trees and a colonnaded cloister. This scheme was also common on the front of the house, with a covered, columned walkway at ground level and a balcony on the first floor. The balconies are made of wood and often elaborately decorated. There are a few good examples of this style in the older part of Teguise, the ancient capital of Lanzarote, but due to the lack of timber on the island, wooden balconies are not as common here as they are on the western part of the archipelago. Artisans' houses from this period are much simpler stone and whitewashed buildings, with predominantly flat roofs. There is a simple way to date the older houses in Lanzarote – up to the end of the 17th century, windows were often placed at irregular levels, but from the 17th century onwards, house façades became symmetrical, with a door at the centre and equal-sized and spaced windows. By the 16th century, the *Mudéjar* style

Above: *An old traditional door in need of attention.*
Opposite: *Dancers in local costume at a festival in Teguise.*

CARNIVAL

The **carnaval** at Arrecife is a highlight on the island's calendar. Mostly held along the waterfront promenade, the carnival lasts for two weeks during February and is a riot of music, dancing and fireworks. It traditionally ends with the Ceremony of the Dying Sardine (*see* panel, page 28). Another lively carnival is held at Puerto del Carmen – all the settlements on the island join in the fun in their own small way.

Above: *Traditional carved wooden balconies at Teguise.*
Opposite: *A striking mural at the César Manrique Foundation.*

had been replaced by the intricate *Plateresque*, named after the work of silversmiths and particularly evident in carved doorways and ceilings. By the 19th century, **Portuguese Baroque** had appeared – typified by iron railings on balconies. During the same period public buildings, such as town halls and museums, were being constructed in the **Neoclassical** style. The early 20th century saw some interesting **Art Nouveau** buildings which were mainly the work of César Manrique. The second half of the century saw the growth of tourism in the Canary Islands and with it came some unattractive multi-storeyed apartment blocks. Fortunately, Manrique saw to it that Lanzarote largely resisted the spread of these eyesores.

The Influence of César Manrique

The remarkable César Manrique is undoubtedly Lanzarote's best-known son. He was born in Arrecife in 1919, but grew up in La Caleta de Famara on the northern coast of the island. He became a celebrated modern artist and worked abroad for many years, both in mainland Spain and in New York. When he returned to Lanzarote in the 1960s he was appalled at the development that had taken place on the island. He devoted the rest of his life to educating his fellow *Lanzaroteños* about the harmony of art, nature and landscape in order to prevent the unsightly development that was threatening his homeland. He had considerable influence over the island's *cabildo* (town council) and managed to prevent high-rise buildings, so that no structure (except church towers) is built higher than a Canary palm. He recommended that rural buildings have whitewashed walls, with green doors and window frames. Roadside

FINDING A TOILET

Public toilets are non-existent in Lanzarote, but this is not a problem. Most people just nip into a restaurant or bar to use the facilities – it is normal practice and you do not have to be a customer. Toilet doors have the usual easily recognizable male and female signs. Do use the toilets when visiting any of the César Manrique institutions, as they are among the most luxurious and civilized that you will find anywhere in the world. In particular, do not miss the amazing male and female signs on the toilet doors at Manrique's Cactus Garden (see page 77).

hoardings were banned, as was the tipping of rubbish, while all electric cables were to be laid underground.

Manrique also made his own artistic contributions to the landscape. His sculptures and mobiles (such as that of **Monumento al Campesino**, situated near Mozaga) grace the scenery. He turned the caves at **Jameos del Agua** and the **Cueva de los Verdes** from foul-smelling rubbish tips into places of unique beauty, designed a remarkable restaurant on the **Islote de Hilario** volcano, converted the **Castillo de San José** at Arrecife into an art gallery and restaurant, and designed the extraordinary **Mirador del Río** with its fantastic views across to Isla Graciosa. Manrique was also responsible for the **Cactus Garden** at Guatiza. Typically, he wanted no financial recompense for his effort and was quite happy just to see visitors as well as *Lanzaroteños* appreciate the unspoilt beauty of the island.

When Manrique moved to Haría in 1988 he presented his former home at Taro de Tahiche to the public. This remarkable villa was built within a series of huge volcanic bubbles. It is now the Manrique Foundation (*see* page 79) and is open to visitors. Manrique was tragically killed in a car accident in 1992 at the age of 72, but his achievements live on for all to appreciate.

MALPAÍS

Large parts of southern Lanzarote are covered with black lava flows and cinders known as ***malpaís*** or **badlands**. Despite the fact that many of these lava flows are nearly 300 years old they are almost completely devoid of vegetation. The reason for this is the climate. Lanzarote's arid weather, with little rain and no frost, has been unable to break down the rock into a soil. The only plants to be seen are lichens. Over a hundred species of these have been identified, with the white *sterocalum* being the most common. The spreads of black *picón* fare a little better with occasional clumps of euphorbia of the *tabaibales* family. Comparisons with the surface of the moon are not far-fetched!

2
Arrecife

In Guanche times the coastal areas of Lanzarote were frequently raided by Berbers from North Africa and people were taken away to be used as slaves. The situation continued after the Spanish Conquest with the additional hazard of pirate raids from Spain's seafaring enemies. For this reason the capital of the island was located inland, at Teguise, where the inhabitants were safer. By the 19th century the island was a lot more peaceful due to its close links with the Americas. It was now important for a coastal town to be the main administrative settlement of the island. Thus, in 1824, Arrecife became the capital, although it is still known to locals as El Puerto. Arrecife (which means reef) gets its name from the numerous reefs of volcanic rock that lie offshore and protect the port.

Today, Arrecife is a typical Spanish working town and port with nearly 40,000 inhabitants, many of whom travel to work at the main tourist resorts daily. Although it is not a particularly attractive place, Arrecife does not have the spread of high-rise apartment blocks which disfigure many Spanish cities. Instead, the suburbs consist mainly of single-storeyed houses in either a Canarian or Andalucían style. The town centre, however, is not particularly distinguished and few travel agents bother to arrange trips to Arrecife, although – for the more independent traveller with a hired car – the capital is well worth at least a half-day visit. It has a busy shopping centre, with shops selling goods at much cheaper prices than those in the resorts. It also has a couple of ancient

DON'T MISS

*** Castillo de San José: explore the castle that has been converted into a world-class modern art gallery by César Manrique.
** Castillo de San Gabriel: visit the archaeological museum that was once a defense fortress.
* Charco de San Ginés: view a tidal inlet stretching into the heart of the town, lined with bars and shops.
* Iglesia de San Ginés: have a look at Arrecife's charming parish church.

Opposite: *Small fishing boats in Arrecife's tidal Charco de San Ginés.*

CLIMATE

Arrecife has a good climate all year round, with little rain. Sea breezes cool the summer heat, but visitors would do well to avoid the town when the sirocco wind blows from Africa.

castles, a few museums and art galleries, an interesting parish church, and a tidal lagoon that extends right into the middle of the town. The seafront, with its gardens and promenade, encourages an enjoyable stroll.

A word of warning for visitors arriving here by car – Arrecife is the only place on the island that has a traffic problem. Jams are common on the narrow roads around the town centre and parking can be very difficult. The best place to park is right next to Castillo de San Gabriel on the seafront. Parking is free, although the efficient self-appointed parking attendants usually deserve a tip. Arrive before 09:30 or you will find the car park full. The tourist office is on the seafront adjacent to the car park, and they provide a helpful town plan.

THE CENTRE

Castillo de San Gabriel **

A convenient first stop is the **Castillo de San Gabriel**, which is approached from Avenida Generalísimo Franco on the seafront by two causeways, one for traffic and the other for pedestrians. The castle, which was originally a wooden fortress, is actually built on a small rocky island called the Islote de los Ingleses. It was certainly not adequate to repel invaders, as it was eventually burnt down by Berber pirates. The castle was replaced in 1572 by a stone castle built by the Spaniard Sancho de Selín. It was reinforced in 1586 and again in 1590, but still found to be defective. Eventually it was completely rebuilt in 1592, during the reign of Felipe II, to the plans of the Italian fortress builder Leonardo Torriani (*see* panel, page 45).

Outside the castle, which is built with a pretty honey-coloured stone, are a couple of rusty old cannons. Inside is a modest archaeological museum, displaying pottery,

Arrecife

0 — 500 m
0 — 500 yd

CASTILLO DE SAN JOSÉ

Valterra

Santa Coloma

La Vega

Charco de San Ginés

La Destilla

Playa del Reducto

Puerto de Naos

1. Instituto de Formación Profesional
2. Instituto de Bachillerato Blas Cabrera Felipe
3. Escuela de Artes y Oficios Artísticos Pancho Lasso
4. Hospital Insular de Arrecife
5. Ayuntamiento
6. Iglesia de San Ginés
7. Miramar Hotel
8. Puenta de las Bolas
9. Casa de la Cultura
10. Castillo de San Gabriel
11. El Almacén
12. Cruz Roja
13. Parque Islas Canarias
14. Gran Hotel
15. Lancelot Hotel
16. Cabildo de Lanzarote

Left: *Calle León y Castillo – the main pedestrian shopping street in Arrecife.*

fossils, coins, primitive jewellery and a few skeletons and skulls dating back to Guanche times. The narrow passageways allow one to observe the thickness of Torriani's walls, and it is also possible to go up onto the roof, from which there is a fine view over the town. The museum's opening times are erratic and there is a small entrance fee.

From the castle's roof the skyline is dominated by the tall structure of the **Gran Hotel**. This is the only building on the island resembling a skyscraper. It was built while César Manrique was overseas and he was horrified by the sight on his return. He did not want further constructions of this kind on the rest of the island, so he

---

LEÓN Y CASTILLO

All the major towns of the Canary Islands seem to have a street or plaza named **León y Castillo**. Arrecife is no exception, since its main shopping street bears this name. Where did the name come from? It originates from two brothers who contributed a lot to the islands during their careers in the 19th and early 20th centuries. Fernando León y Castillo was a diplomat and politician who rose to the position of Foreign Minister of Spain and while in this job, he was able to obtain many dispensations for the islands. His brother, Juan, was an engineer and designed many projects in the Canaries. Their family home in Gran Canaria is now a museum.

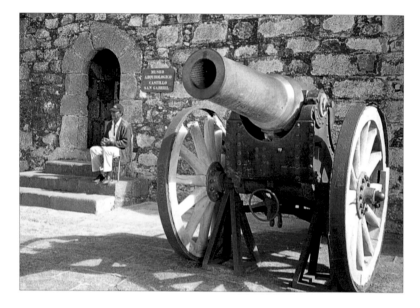

persuaded the island's government to allow him to over-see future building developments on Lanzarote. The Gran Hotel was partially destroyed by a fire in 1994 and at the time of writing it remains derelict, standing out like a sore thumb as a constant reminder of developers' greed.

Puente de las Bolas

Returning to the shore via the pedestrian causeway, you pass under the **Puente de las Bolas** (The Bridge of the Cannonballs), an old drawbridge named after the cannonballs on the top of its pillars. It has been adopted as the emblem of Lanzarote. Along the shoreline there are attractive gardens, known as the Parque José Ramírez Cerdá, with Canary palms (in which little egrets roost in the evenings), bougainvilleas and other colour-ful shrubs. The helpful **Oficina de Turismo** is located here in a pleasant kiosk.

Immediately opposite the bridge is Arrecife's main shopping street, Calle León y Castillo. Pedestrianized, it has most of the town's banks and a full range of shops, bars and restaurants, as well as the Centro Commercial Atlantida, which contains Lanzarote's largest department store. The island's *cabildo* (town council), with its attractive tiled frontage, is located on the right-hand side of Calle Léon y Castillo.

Iglesia de San Ginés *

Turn right immediately after the *cabildo* along a narrow lane that leads to the shady square, the Plaza de Las Palmas. Here we find the parish church, the **Iglesia de San Ginés**. It was originally a 17th-century hermitage and became the parish church in 1798, dedicated to San Ginés, the patron saint of Arrecife.

The exterior is a pleasing combination of dark volcanic stone and whitewash, and the impressive square tower is capped with a belfry in the form of a gleaming white cupola. It is the dominant landmark of the town. The interior of the church is also full of interest. Simple black basalt columns lead to round arches of red volcanic material. The dark wooden ceiling is crafted in *Mudéjar* style, and the delicately painted pulpit with its spiral staircase is also made of wood. It is impossible to miss the symbolic modern painting, by Alberto Manrique;

> **NOT JUST A FORTRESS BUILDER**
>
> After continual raids by Berber pirates, Felipe II of Spain decided that the defences of the Canary Islands needed to be re-organized. He turned for assistance to the noted Genoese engineer and fortress builder **Leonardo Torriani**. Among the castles that he built or renovated on Lanzarote were the Castillo de San Gabriel in Arrecife and the Castillo de Santa Bárbara, built on the edge of a volcano overlooking Teguise. Torriani was not just an engineer, however, but also an observant historian. His book, *The Canary Islands and their Original Inhabitants* (1590), includes some wonderful descriptions and illustrations of the Guanches and their way of life. He also wrote a vivid account of the eruption of the Tegueso volcano on the island of La Palma.

Opposite: *A cannon guards the entrance to Castillo de San Gabriel, which is now a museum.*
Left: *Gran Hotel Arrecife. This unused hotel, which was partially destroyed by fire in 1994, is the only skyscraper on the island.*

ASSISTANCE FROM YOUR CONSULATE

Most people will have a trouble-free holiday in Lanzarote. Occasionally, however, a tourist may have a problem and his or her consulate might have to be contacted. Embassies and consulates are limited in the help that they can provide in the Canary Islands. The consulate **can** issue emergency passports, contact relatives and next-of-kin and provide legal help, but they **cannot** pay your bills, investigate crimes or obtain work permits. The nearest British consulate is in Las Palmas on Gran Canaria (tel: 928 262508) and an office is open at the Hotel Los Fariones in Puerto del Carmen (see page 106) during February, May, August and November.

located behind the font, it depicts the fountain of life. It is also worth taking a quick look in the sacristy, where there is a large collection of religious statues. The church, and also the square outside it, are at the centre of the activities during Corpus Christi at Whitsun and the fiesta of San Ginés in August.

On returning to the Avenida Generalísimo Franco, we find a number of important buildings, including the *Ayuntamiento* (or town hall), the Miramar Hotel, and the police station. Also on the waterfront is the **Casa de los Arroyo**, which houses the Blas Cabrera Museum dedicated to the work of the well-known atomic scientist who was born in Arrecife. A small art gallery displays the work of local artist Pancho Lasso. The museum is open from Monday to Friday (10:30–13:30 and 16:30–19:30) and admission is free.

A side street leads to the town's *mercado*, a market selling fruit and vegetables, while on the opposite side of the road is a fascinating fish market.

Charco de San Ginés *

Further east is Arrecife's most attractive scenic feature, **Charco de San Ginés**, a tidal lagoon reaching into the heart of the town. It is said that San Ginés lived as a hermit on its shore. At low tide, wading birds prod among the mud and rocks, while at high tide colourful boats bob against the reflection of the buildings in the water, providing the opportunity to take beautiful photos. A promenade runs right around the *charco* (pool), lined with palm trees, restaurants, bars and souvenir shops. The large modern building at the far end of the *charco* is a multi-screen cinema.

Manrique enthusiasts may want to seek out **El Almacén**, in Calle José Betancort, just off the western end of the Avenida Generalísimo Franco. This building was an old storehouse that César Manrique converted into an art gallery. It also has a bar, restaurant and bookshop.

THE EAST OF THE TOWN
Castillo de San José ★★★
Arrecife's other sightseeing location requires some transport to reach. This is the **Castillo de San José** located in the east of the town. En route you will pass the port, and the first section is the **Puerto de Naos**, which is the harbour for fishing boats. Arrecife has the largest fishing fleet in the Canary Islands and the seventh-largest in Spain. Fish is the basis of both the local canning and salting industries. You then reach the main commercial docks, the **Puerto de los Mármoles**,

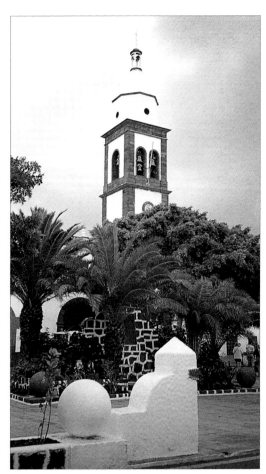

Above: *Iglesia de San Ginés, the parish church of Arrecife.*
Opposite: *Puente de las Bolas, the Bridge of the Cannonballs, has become Lanzarote's emblem.*

Above: *Charco de San Ginés, a tidal lagoon running into the heart of Arrecife.*
Opposite: *The Castillo de San José was converted by César Manrique into a museum of modern art.*

SEEING IN THE NEW YEAR

It is the habit in Spain, including Lanzarote, to celebrate the New Year rather than Christmas. At the stroke of midnight on New Year's Eve it is the custom to drink *cava* (the Spanish version of champagne) and eat a grape for each strike of the clock. To consume 12 grapes and take a drink so quickly is not easy and it usually leads to great hilarity.

---

which is the second-largest port in the Canaries after Las Palmas and deals mainly in the container trade.

The **Castillo de San José** was built between 1776 and 1779, on the orders of King Carlos III, partly with the aim of defending the port against pirates. More importantly, it served to provide work and money for the *Lanzaroteños*, who had been suffering from starvation after the volcanic eruptions earlier in the century had destroyed their farmland. For this reason the castle became known as the *Fortaleza del Hambre* – the Hunger Fortress. For many years it acted as a powder and ammunition store, but by the 20th century it had become derelict. In 1968 César Manrique suggested that it should be renovated and converted into an art gallery. Work soon began and in 1976 it was opened as the **Museo Internacional de Arte Contemporáneo**. Manrique put together a collection of abstract art, including work by Tápies, Picasso, Miró and of course his own pictures, along with modern sculptures, many of which are outside the entrance.

The castle has proved to be a unique setting for an art gallery, with the dark barrel-like ceilings of the 18th-century building contrasting with the bright and colourful paintings and sculptures. A spiral staircase leads down to Manrique's restaurant, the design of which he is said to have drawn directly onto the ground with chalk! The restaurant has dramatically modern black tables and chairs, and even black napkins, while a huge picture window looks out over the bustling container docks. As is usual with Manrique's schemes, the toilets are well worth a visit, with classical music accompanying your ablutions.

The Castillo de San José is open daily (11:00–21:00) and so is the restaurant (11:00–24:00). Admission to the castle is free and buses run at half-hourly intervals from the Arrecife waterfront.

THE TOWN BEACHES

After a morning's sightseeing in Arrecife, what better way to spend the afternoon than to visit the town beaches – the **Playa del Reducto** and the **Playa del Cable**. They stretch from the town all the way to the airport and have been cleaned up to such an extent that they have earned Blue Flags.

> ### THE VIRGEN DEL CARMEN FESTIVALS
>
> The Virgen del Carmen is the patron saint of fishermen and seafarers. Each July the fishing villages around the coast of Lanzarote honour this saint with a spectacular festival. An image of the virgin is taken from the parish church and paraded around the streets, ending up at the beach or harbour. Here, she is briefly taken into the sea, either on the shoulders of the fishermen or on a boat, before being taken back to her sanctuary. The fiesta is accompanied by singing, dancing, fireworks and the cooking of giant paellas.

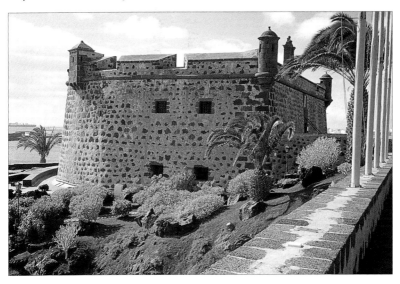

Arrecife at a Glance

BEST TIMES TO VISIT

Arrecife is pleasant place to visit at any time of the year, although a particularly interesting time to go to the capital is during the **Fiesta de San Ginés**, which takes place in the month of August and lasts for approximately a week. Also in August is the **Fiesta del Carmen**, when the celebrations include effigies of the saint being floated on the sea.

GETTING THERE

Regular **buses** run from the resorts to Arrecife, but they are not always very reliable. **Taxis** are cheap, but hired **cars** are generally more convenient. The best place to park your car is alongside the Castillo San Gabriel in the seafront. Try to arrive early, as the parking area becomes congested quickly. The tourist information office is conveniently situated next to the car park.

GETTING AROUND

The most attractive and interesting features of Arrecife are within walking distance from the main car park, although transport is necessary to visit Castillo de San José. Buses in the area run at half-hourly intervals and taxis are also available. The main taxi rank is situated opposite the Castillo de San Gabriel. There are other taxi ranks in Calle León y Castillo and Calle Pérez Galdós. For Radio Taxi, tel: 928 803104. The bus station is in Vía Medular.

WHERE TO STAY

Few tourists stay in Arrecife, as it is not necessary with the major resorts situated close by. Accommodation here is rather limited and generally caters for business people. Hotels on Lanzarote, as in the rest of the Islands, are given a star rating based on the various facilities that are offered and not the quality.

MID-RANGE

Hotel Lancelot, Avenida Mancomunidad 9, tel: 928 805099, fax: 928 805089. A modern hotel overlooking the beach, with both a pool and a bar.
Hotel Miramar, Avenida Coll 2, tel: 928 801522, fax: 928 803366. A very convenient, seafront location.

BUDGET

Inspect the room before making a reservation.
Pensión Alepsa, Calle Léon y Castillo 56, tel: 928 811756. Simple, clean and situated close to the centre of town.
Pensión Cardona, Calle 18 Julio 11, tel: 928 811008, fax: 928 817008. Large hostel, central and close to the seafront.
Pensión España, Calle Gran Canaria 4, tel: 928 811190. Situated close to the shopping centre and the *charco*.
Pensión Arrocha, Avenida de León y Castillo 98, tel: 928 802421. A very clean, neat and comfortable place to stay.
Hotel Residencia San Ginés, Calle del Molino 9, tel: 928 811 863. Another reasonably priced and rather cheerful option that is available to visitors.

WHERE TO EAT

There is a good range of traditional Canarian and international restaurants, but few genuine *tapas* bars remain in Arrecife.

LUXURY

Castillo de San José, tel: 928 812321. Sophisticated food is served at this Manrique-designed restaurant in a converted castle overlooking the harbour. It is recommended that you make reservations well in advance.

MID-RANGE

Marisquería Mesón Los Troncos, Calle Agustin de la Hoz 9, tel: 928 813637. A restaurant serving outstanding seafood, next to the Puerto de Naos.
Ciao, Calle La Esperanza 1, tel: 928 813511. Opposite the seafront gardens. Very good pizzas and typical Canarian dishes.
Lancelot, Avenida Mancomunidad 9,

Arrecife at a Glance

tel: 928 805090. A hotel restaurant opposite El Reducto beach.

Taiwan, Calle Canalejas 52, tel: 928 814562. A moderately priced Chinese restaurant.

Casa Ginory, Calle Juan de Quesada 7, tel: 928 804046. A good seafood restaurant located close to the *charco*.

El Almirante, Playa del Cable, tel: 928 805985. A beachside restaurant offering a very large variety of food on their menu.

Marisquería Abdon, Calle Canalejas 54, tel: 928 814558. A fish bar as well as a takeaway service situated in the city centre.

BUDGET

Tapas Bars
One of the finest, and certainly the one with the best ambience, is **San Francisco**, Calle León y Castillo 10, inside an atmospheric cellar. Other *tapas* bars include **Lemon Bar** and **Café Bar Minoca** alongside the *charco*. Visitors with a sweet tooth should try the **Pastelería Lolita**, which is just opposite the casino.

SHOPPING

Arrecife is probably the best place to shop on the island. Shops are centred along Calle León y Castillo and its side streets. The prices here are a lot more reasonable than in the resorts. There is

a Saturday morning market alongside El Charco de San Ginés. Manrique fans can buy goods with his designs and prints at the Tienda Fundación César Manrique, Calle José Betancourt 26. Local craftworks can be found in a number of artisan shops in the area. The best bookshop in Arrecife is Librería el Puente in Calle Insp. Luis Martín.

USEFUL CONTACTS

Oficina de Turismo, Parque Municipal, tel: 928 811762. The office is open weekdays (10:00–14:00 and 17:00–20:00) and on Saturday (10:00–14:00).
A number of firms offering adventure sports are based in Arrecife and their activities include:
Hang-gliding, Clube de Parapente Los Cuervos, tel: 928 815426; and Delta Club Zonzamas, tel: 928 815203.
Water-skiing, Nautic Boat, tel: 928 800007. This firm also offers **fishing** trips.
Skydiving, contact Lanzarote Skydive Centre,

tel: 928 840114.
Windsurfing, Club de Windsurf Los Charcos, tel: 928 810894.
Diving, try the Club de Actividades Subacuaticas Pastinaca based at Playa Monda, which is to the south of Arrecife.
The **main post office** is situated at Avenida Generalísimo Franco 8.
In the event of an **emergency** contact the main police station at Avenida del Coll 5, tel: 928 812350.
For **medical emergencies** call the Red Cross, tel: 928 812212.
The **main hospital** is situated on the northwest side of the town on the San Bartolomé road.

ENTERTAINMENT

Arrecife can be quite lively in the evenings, with a number of clubs and bars along Calle José Antonio offering live music. One of the trendiest spots is **La Naos** in Avenida de Naos opposite the port.
Teatro Atlantico located on the shore of the *charco* is a multi-screen cinema.

ARRECIFE	J	F	M	A	M	J	J	A	S	O	N	D
AVERAGE TEMP. °F	63	66	68	70	77	77	79	79	79	77	72	66
AVERAGE TEMP. °C	17	19	20	21	25	25	26	26	26	25	22	19
HUMIDITY %	81	82	80	81	81	80	80	79	81	82	83	84
RAINFALL in	2	0	0.4	0.3	0	0	0	0	0	1.7	0.1	0.1
RAINFALL mm	51	1	12	7	0	0	0	0	0	42	2	3
DAYS OF SUN	18	16	20	18	18	16	13	12	17	18	17	16

3
The North and the Islands

Scenically, the north of Lanzarote is the most fascinating part of the island. Like the south, it has areas where there has been recent volcanic activity, with large stretches of volcanic lava forming *malpaís*, but in general the eruptions happened earlier in historical time, so the lava and ash have had time to mature and form a reasonable soil. Farming in the north also benefits from a higher level of precipitation, as the area catches rain from the northerly trade winds.

There are also plenty of tourist attractions which include the famous tubes that formed in the lava flows from Mount Corona. The **Jameos del Agua**, adapted imaginatively by César Manrique, and the **Cueva de los Verdes**, where the Guanches used to hide from Berber pirates, both attract coach loads of visitors throughout the year. Manrique was also responsible for developing the **Mirador del Río**, which affords superb views of **Isla Graciosa** and the other islands to the north. There are two more *miradors* providing wonderful vistas at Guinate and Haría.

Although there are no large tourist resorts in the north of the island, there are a number of small fishing villages, such as **Arrieta** and **Orzola**, where delicious seafood can be found in restaurants with terraces looking out over the Atlantic. Orzola also provides a ferry service to Isla Graciosa. Despite the fact that most holidaymakers will be based in resorts in southern Lanzarote, they should make an effort to visit the north with its superb scenery and Manrique-inspired restaurants.

DON'T MISS

*** Jameos del Agua: Manrique's conversion of volcanic tubes into an concert hall, nightclub and pools.
*** Cueva de los Verdes: volcanic tubes under lava.
*** Mirador del Río: look-out point and restaurant designed by Manrique.
** Mirador de Guinate: viewpoint overlooking El Río and Isla de Graciosa.
** Mirador de Haría: a pass with magnificent views.
** Parque Tropical: over 1300 species of birds and animals.

Opposite: *Visitors stroll around Jameos del Agua, Manrique's conversion of volcanic tubes and bubbles.*

ARRIETA AND SURROUNDS

The road north from Arrecife meets the coast at **Arrieta**, a small, unpretentious fishing village. The roundabout at the entrance to the village is graced by a striking red wind sculpture by César Manrique, and the area in the vicinity is now seeing a modest amount of development. Arrieta has a small harbour and an equally small sandy beach called the **Playa de la Garita**. Here there are several fish restaurants that tempt the visitor, but prices are not cheap. Another reason to linger in Arrieta is the **Centro de Arte y Cultura Africana** (the Museum of African Art and Culture) located in a building sometimes known as the Blue House. The Museum has a collection of African artefacts and pictures, but it was closed for renovation at the time of writing.

Just north of Arrieta is a small, and quite unspoilt, fishing settlement called **Punta de Mujeres**. This village marks the start of the **Malpaís de la Corona**, an area of badlands that stretches north for the next 10km (6.2 miles) to Orzola. This volcanic lava flowed out of **Mount Corona**, which can be seen to the west, rising to some 609m (2000ft). Although the eruption took place between 5000 and 6000 years ago, there is remarkably little vegetation on the surface of the lava, apart from white lichens and a few clumps of spurges. The *malpaís* is famous for being the location of one of the longest **lava tubes** in the world. The tube runs southeast from the volcano for 7.5km (4.7 miles), and the last 1km (0.6 mile) is under the sea bed. Occasionally the tube widens out and forms 'bubbles' or caves. These include two of the most popular tourist attractions on the island.

Above: *Lobster sculpture at the entrance to the Jameos del Agua.*

The Jameos del Agua ★★★

This complex of caves and partially collapsed tubes has been adapted by César Manrique to form the most remarkable showpiece on Lanzarote. Just outside the complex is a huge sculpture of a lobster, similar to the illustration in Torriani's 16th-century book. A few steps at the entrance lead down into a bar that doubles as a nightclub on certain evenings of the week. The route leads into a large cavern containing a salt-water lake, thought to be the water that has filtered through the rocks. The lake's only inhabitants are small, blind, albino crabs (*Munidopsis polymorpha*) that average 3mm (0.12in) in length. How they got into the cave is unclear

> **CLIMATE**
>
> There is the possibility of light rain and even mist on the hills during the winter months when it can be quite cool, but for the rest of the year it should be warm and dry. The north is windier than the south of the island, particularly during the hotter summer months.

Right: *Lush vegetation surrounds this pool at Jameos del Agua, one of Lanzarote's most popular attractions.*

as their normal habitat is in deep-sea water. A notice requests that you do not throw coins in the water as the copper can adversely affect the crabs. Emerging from the cavern, you enter a contrasting world of lush plants, including palms and bougainvilleas, set around a deep blue pool with whitewashed surrounds. It is said that the King of Spain is the only person allowed to swim in the pool. At the far end of the pool is another cavern containing an auditorium with 550 seats, which is frequently used for concerts and shows. The whole place is awe-inspiring and many visitors feel the need to sit for a while and contemplate, while they soak up the atmosphere of this unusual location. Back at the poolside, zig-zagged steps lead up to a terrace with a café, a small museum (the Casa de Volcanes) and more remarkable Manrique toilets. Before leaving this extraordinary place, spare a moment and take the path over the *malpaís* down to the ocean, observing how plants are struggling to survive among the hostile lava. The Jameos del Agua are open daily (09:30–19:00), with reduced hours in the winter. The restaurant is open on Tuesday, Friday and Saturday (19:00–03:00) as a nightclub, with occasional folklore performances.

Cueva de los Verdes ★★★

A short distance away is the rival attraction, **Cueva de los Verdes**. The word *verde* means green in Spanish, but there is nothing green about the cave – it was once owned by people by the name of Verde. Tour guides often, in fact, call it Green's cave. The whole place is a complex of caves at various levels, opening out into occasional caverns, one of which is large enough to host concerts – although one is mystified as to how the musicians get some of their bulkier instruments through the narrow tunnels. These caves are unlike those in limestone areas, which are often dripping with water and festooned with stalactites and stalagmites. Their attraction lies in the colour of the volcanic rocks, accentuated by clever lighting and atmospheric music. The caves have been known about for many centuries and they were used by local people to hide from invaders, such as pirates and slave traders. The Cueva de los Verdes is open daily (10:00–19:00). Guided tours run half-hourly and last for about an hour. The walk is quite demanding in places.

> **LAVA TUBES**
>
> When volcanic lava is of the thick and viscous kind, such as that which flowed out of Mount Corona and formed the *malpaís* of northeastern Lanzarote, **volcanic tubes** can be quite common. They are formed when the surface lava cools, but at lower levels the lava continues to flow and eventually leaves a cave-like tube or pipe behind. These tubes can frequently be followed for many kilometres and often widen out into large caverns.

Below: *The Cueva de los Verdes is a complex of caves and caverns located in a lava flow.*

Below: *Small boats surround the Isla Graciosa ferry at Orzola Harbour.*

ORZOLA

The coast road continues northwards through the *malpaís*. If cars are parked by the roadside, this usually indicates that there is a secluded beach nearby. The sand in these coves is light in colour and makes a striking contrast with the dark volcanic rocks. The road eventually arrives at **Orzola**, the most northerly village in Lanzarote. It is a sleepy fishing settlement and noted for its seafood restaurants, many of which have terraces overlooking the harbour. Reefs of volcanic rock protect the harbour and this is not a safe area to swim or dive in rough weather. There is a good sandy beach, however, just to the north called Playa de la Cantería. Ferries run three or four times a day from Orzola to Isla Graciosa.

Las Pardelas

The road to Mirador del Río runs to the southwest out of Orzola. On the outskirts of the town is **Las Pardelas**, a sort of recreational and ecological park, offering indigenous flora, traditional craft demonstrations – including the making of *gofio* – and also animal rides. The appeal here is largely to children. It is open daily (10:00–18:00) and there is a small restaurant.

YÉ AND SURROUNDS

A spectacular mountain road now leads across to the town of Yé. This strange place name appears to have meant 'the end of the earth' in the Guanche language. It was once an important centre for extracting purple dye from lichen, but today its main claim to fame is the remarkable skill of its wrestlers.

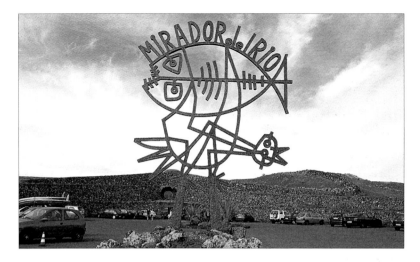

Mirador del Río ★★★

We now reach another of Lanzarote's locations that cannot be missed, the **Mirador del Río**. This, again, is the work of César Manrique. In 1974, with his typical flair, he converted an old gun emplacement some 497m (1630ft) above sea level into a restaurant and viewing platform. From the car park the place initially looks uninspiring, with a drab convex curve of volcanic block merging into the hillside, but – inside – a narrow passage leads to a restaurant, dominated by two of Manrique's ceiling sculptures. Picture windows lead to a semi-circular viewing platform providing one of the best vistas in the Canary Islands. Down beneath the steep cliffs is the abandoned saltworks of the **Salinas del Río**, with its subtle pink water. Then, further out, is **El Río**, which is not a river at all, but the strait that separates Isla Graciosa from the mainland. The island itself looks barren, with just one small settlement, **Caleta del Sebo**, some sand dunes and a few extinct volcanoes. Away in the distance other islands can be seen, such as **Montaña Clara** and **Alegranza**, which are inhabited only by sea birds. It is necessary to pay for entrance to the *mirador*, which is open daily (10:00–18:00).

Above: *Another striking Manrique sculpture marks the entrance to the Mirador del Río.*

TREASURE ISLAND

Isla Graciosa, to the north of Lanzarote, is dry and barren. It is many people's idea of the archetypal desert island. So perhaps it is inevitable that there are stories of buried treasure on Isla Graciosa. One such tale concerns an English ship that was chased to the island by pirates. The crew managed to bury their treasure before they were killed. However, the ship's cabin boy survived and fled back to England. He never revealed the location of the treasure until he was very old, but by then he was too senile to remember the exact spot.

Above: *A peacock struts his stuff at the Parque Tropical at Guinate.*
Opposite: *Haría is a pleasant town in the 'valley of a thousand palms'.*

GUINATE

Mirador de Guinate **

If you don't like the idea of paying the entrance fee to the Mirador del Río, then all is not lost – head southwards to the village of **Guinate**. Turn right and proceed towards the sea. Just past the Parque Tropical is the **Mirador de Guinate**, which has no entrance fee and arguably provides even better views than does the Mirador del Río. Look out for the hang-gliders and paragliders, who enjoy the updraughts caused by the winds beating against the towering cliffs of the **Risco de Famara**.

Parque Tropical **

The other reason for stopping at Guinate is to visit the **Parque Tropical**. Covering some 45,000m^2, the park claims to have over 1300 rare and exotic birds and animals. Many birds breed in the large aviaries, while others, such as peacocks, roam free. There is a huge walk-through aviary and in the lush vegetation you can see weaver birds busily building their hanging nests. There are numerous streams, waterfalls and ponds full of enormous koi carp. The park also has some monkeys and lemurs, having been brought here after being rescued from illegal owners. A firm favourite with children is the parrot show, which is held six times a day. These colourful birds (actually sulphur crested cockatoos and blue macaws) perform tricks such as pulling toy carts, driving model pick-up trucks and riding toy bicycles. Parque Tropical is open daily (10:00–17:00), although the admission fee is pricey. There is a large free car park halfway between the park and the *mirador*.

HARÍA

The road continues southwards to **Haría**, which is the main town of northern Lanzarote and certainly one of the most attractive villages on the island. Part of its allure is the unexpected abundance of trees, and tour guides often refer to the area as the 'valley of a thousand palms'. A local legend suggests that a palm tree was planted for every girl born here and two for each boy, but the truth may be more prosaic – the palms are most probably the remains of a 16th-century plantation. Haría and the surrounding valley certainly look green and fertile, particularly after the winter rains which produce a wealth of wild flowers. The town itself has around 3000 inhabitants and is full of interest, with its numerous craft shops where artisans can be seen at work. It does not come as a surprise to learn that César Manrique chose to retire in Haría. One oddity is the **Museo Internacional de Miniaturas** (the Museum of Miniatures) which contains some remarkable exhibition articles, such as a football match painted on a grain of rice, and what claims to be the smallest bible in the world. The museum is open daily (10:00–19:00) and the

THE WILD CANARY

Despite the fact that Lanzarote is one of the Canary Islands, your chances of seeing a wild canary are rather slim. The wild ancestor of the familiar bright yellow canary singing in its cage is endemic to Madeira, the Azores and the Canary Islands. In the wild it is a drab bird, with striated markings and only a touch of dull yellow-green. Only the male sings and its trilling bears little resemblance to that of the captive bird. It can be seen in a variety of habitats, usually near cultivated fields or pine forests where it builds its nest. Clearly Lanzarote does not have the ideal countryside for the canary, but there are rumours that it may have been introduced to the island in recent years.

admission fee is small. A rather more traditional museum is the **Museo de Arte Sacro** attached to the modern parish church in the shady Plaza León y Castillo.

Mirador de Haría **

For the best view of the town of Haría, travel south-wards and climb the pass that leads to the **Mirador de Haría**. There are two bar/restaurants that are popular stops for coaches, and both give spectacular vistas. The great number of palm trees in and around Haría can easily be picked out. Away to the east is the broad valley of Temisa, with a number of abandoned terraces on its flanks, leading down to Tabayesco and Arrieta on the coast. To the south there is the obtrusive hulk of **Peñas del Chache**, which at a height of 670m (2198ft) is Lanzarote's highest mountain.

A DAY TRIP TO ISLA GRACIOSA

For anyone looking for a spot of peace and quiet, a day trip to Isla Graciosa is an interesting possibility. The

Below: *Part of the attractive town of Haría, with some of its many palm trees.*

Left: *The view from the Mirador del Río shows Isla Graciosa, with its complex of volcanoes.*

island was, in fact, Jean de Béthencourt's first landfall in the Canary Islands. He was the Norman who first conquered Lanzarote. Isla Graciosa can be reached by ferry from Orzola and there are three or four daily crossings in both directions by modern launch. The crossing takes 15–30 minutes. There are no roads on Isla Graciosa and therefore no cars, but the main settlement, **Caleta del Sebo**, has a couple of simple *pensiónes* (boarding/guest houses) and some basic restaurants. Lunch at one of these restaurants can be booked in advance when purchasing the ferry ticket. A track links Caleta del Sebo with **Pedro Barba**, the only other settlement on the island. There are only around 600 permanent residents on the island and most of them are involved in fishing. As Isla Graciosa covers a mere 25km² (9.7 square miles), it is quite possible to walk around the island in a day, using the footpath that follows the shore. Mountain bikes can also be hired at the port. The scenery consists largely of deserted sandy beaches, sand dunes, barren plains and the cones of four extinct volcanoes, including Agujas Chicas at 257m (843ft), Agujas Grandes at 266m (872ft), Montaña del Mojón at 188m (606ft) and Montaña Bermeja at 157m (515ft). Isla Graciosa is the perfect place to experience a tranquil day out!

> ### TO TIP OR NOT TO TIP?
>
> It is always important to know whether or not tipping is expected. In the Canary Islands a tip (*una propina*) is always appreciated, but don't pay up unless the service is good. In restaurants, check the bill to see if the service charge is included. If not, it is usual to add between 5 and 10 per cent. In cafés and bars, some loose change is normally sufficient. Porters in airports and hotels generally expect a small tip. On excursions, coach drivers and guides are normally rewarded if they have provided a good service.

The North and the Islands at a Glance

The north is generally cloudier than the south of Lanzarote, so choose a clear day to visit the area. It can also be very breezy as it receives the full force of the trade winds. The northern beaches may be remote and with few people but the blown sand can make things uncomfortable, while the ocean currents can be dangerous, particularly beneath the cliffs of Famara.

Buses travel from Arrecife to Arrieta, Orzola and Haria four times a day and link with the ferry to Isla Graciosa, but the service can be unreliable.
Coach tours visit the major sites, but rarely allow sufficient time for leisurely sightseeing. A hired **car** is most convenient.

The few major roads in the north are in good condition and signposting is clear, so those with hired cars should have few problems. Some minor roads and rough tracks, however, are in poor conditions and should be avoided. Remember that petrol stations can be few and far between.

Good quality accommodation is virtually non-existent in the north of Lanzarote, since both Arrecife and the main southern holiday centres are within reach. There are a few pensiónes on **Isla Graciosa** and a few apartments and bungalows elsewhere.

BUDGET

Pensión Enriqueta, Calle de la Mar Barlovento 6, Caleta del Sebo, tel: 928 842051. Alongside the harbour, with a restaurant.
Pensión Girasol, Harbour, Caleta del Sebo, tel: 928 842 051. There is a restaurant and some rooms with a sea view.
Apartamientos Pescador, tel: 928 842036. Self-catering apartments close to the ferry jetty at Caleta del Sebo.
Casitas del Mar, tel: 928 835199. Small bungalows can be hired at this modest complex just north of Arrieta.
Bungalows Famara, Urbanisación Famara, tel: 928 845132. Rooms for hire at this unobtrusive development on the northwest coast.
For permission to **camp** on Isla Graciosa contact the ayuntamiento in Caleta del Sebo, tel/fax: 928 842000.

There is a wide choice of places to eat in the area, particularly in Arrieta and Orzola. There are also a number of restaurants, mainly inland, where traditional Canarian food can be found.

Arrieta

This small fishing village has a number of excellent restaurants near the harbour.

MID-RANGE

Casa Miguel, Calle de Noria, tel: 928 835225. This well-established quayside restaurant is full of atmosphere. Serves a selection of traditional local seafood.
El Charcón, Calle de Noria, tel: 928 835630. Another quayside restaurant serving traditional dishes.
Miguel's, Calle de la Marina, tel: 928 835225. Harbourside restaurant with a pleasant marine atmosphere.
Restaurant El Ancla, Calle de la Marina. This is another good-quality Arrieta seafood restaurant.
Jameos del Agua, tel: 928 835010. Many visitors to Jameos del Agua will find it convenient to eat here. There is an excellent snack bar open daily and a good restaurant open on Tue, Fri and Sat evenings to coincide with the folklore shows. It is open from 19:00–03:00, with the show taking place at 23:00.

Orzola

The small fishing village and ferry port has plenty of seafood restaurants.

MID-RANGE

Perla del Atlantico, Avenida de Caleton, tel: 928 842525. Harbourside restaurant serves delicious fresh fish.
Punta Fariones, Calle de la Quemadita, tel: 928 842558. Overlooks the ferry quay and provides high-quality fish dishes.

The North and the Islands at a Glance

Bahía de Orzola, Avenida de Caleton. Another good choice for fresh seafood.

BUDGET
Casa Arraez, Avenida de Caleton. Don't be put off by the rustic nature of this establishment. The fish is fresh and the price is a bargain.
There are one or two restaurants away from the harbour. When the main restaurants are full, **El Norte** is worth a try.

Mirador del Río
LUXURY
Mirador del Río, tel: 928 644318. Striking Manrique-designed eatery overlooking Isla Graciosa.

Haría
There are two restaurants on the Mirador del Valle pass, both with superb views to the north.
MID-RANGE
Los Helechos, tel: 928 835 089. Canteen-style eatery, popular with coach parties.
Mirador del Valle, tel: 928 528036. Simple country café with a view, halfway down the pass. Take care, as it is on a dangerous bend.
The town of Haría also has a number of restaurants, many of which serve traditional Canarian dishes.
El Cortijo, Teguise road on the southern edge of the village, tel: 928 835006. This old farmhouse serves traditional food and is popular with the locals.

Los Cascajos, Calle Ferrer 9, Haría, tel: 928 835471. Rural restaurant to the north of the town; produces its own wines.
Casa 'l Cura, Calle Nueva 1, Haría, tel: 928 835556. The local stews are recommended in this rural house.
Restaurante Papa Loca, Plaza Leon y Castillos, tel: 928 835 670. Bargain menu of the day is particularly recommended.
Restaurante Casa Kura, Calle de la Enunción Rodríguez Lasso, Haría. Pricier option on the northern side of the town.

SHOPPING

Artesanía de Haría, Calle Barranco 4, Haría. Good range of the island's craft items, including embroidery, basketware, silverware, pottery and artefacts made from the volcanic rocks and minerals.
Taller de Artesanía, near the southern entrance of the town of Haría. Workshops where potters, woodcarvers, silversmiths and other craftsmen can be seen at work.

TOURS AND EXCURSIONS

All coach tours of the north are arranged by travel operators in the resorts of Costa Teguise, Playa del Carmen and Playa Blanca in the south of the island. A popular tour is entitled 'In the Footsteps of César Manrique'. It visits the **Fundación César Manrique**, the **Cactus Garden**, the **Jameos del Agua** and the **Mirador del Río**. Visitors

with a car could easily duplicate such an excursion.

USEFUL CONTACTS

There are no **Tourist Information Offices** in the north, so brochures and other information will have to be collected from offices in the main southern resorts.
Deep-sea Fishing. Boats for deep-sea fishing and other waterborne activities at Orzola, tel: 928 842558.
Ferry to Isla Graciosa. For details contact **Lineas Martimas Romero**, tel: 928 842070, fax: 982 842069. For information contact the **ferry company** at Calle García Escámez 11, Isla Graciosa. The timetable is as follows:
Summer: Orzola to La Graciosa, 10:00, 12:00, 17:00 and 18:30. La Graciosa to Orzola, 08:00, 11:00, 16:00 and 18:00.
Winter: Orzola to La Graciosa 10:00, 12:00 and 17:00. La Graciosa to Orzola. 08:00, 11:00 and 16:00. Tickets are available at both harbours. The ferry generally takes about 15–30 minutes for the crossing. In very strong winds it may be cancelled.
A service bus from Arrecife connects with the ferry times. No boats run to the tiny uninhabited islands of Roque del Este, Roque del Oeste, Isla de Montaña Clara and Isla de Alegranza. These are offical nature reserves and landing on them is forbidden.

4
Central Lanzarote

Although Central Lanzarote cannot boast the spectacular scenery found in the north and south of the island, the area is full of interest. Right in the centre is **Teguise**, the old capital of Lanzarote, which is full of ancient churches and noble homes. It has a dignified atmosphere, which is disturbed only on Sundays by a market that attracts visitors from all over island.

The coastline of the central area is largely undeveloped, with the notable exception of **Costa Teguise**, a purpose-built resort with Lanzarote's only golf course and aquapark. Fans of **César Manrique** have much to see, with the **Monumento al Campesino**, the **Fundación** in his former home, and the **Cactus Garden** on the outskirts of Guatiza.

Central Lanzarote is also one of the more fertile parts of the island, supporting numerous well-cared-for agricultural villages such as **Mozaga**, famous for its grapes; **Guatiza**, which is the centre of the cochineal industry; and **Tinajo**, specializing in onion and tomato cultivation. Many of these villages have unique and interesting little churches and hermitages. Museums include the award-winning **Museo Agrícola El Patio**, near Tiagua, and the imaginative Manrique-inspired **Casa Museo del Campesino**, near Mozaga. A most surprising feature on the north coast is the world-famous sports complex of **La Santa**, which offers so many sporting activities – such as tennis, sailing, sailboarding and athletics – that it is mentioned in the *Guinness Book of Records*. Many national teams come here to train.

Alegranza Parque Natural de los
Islotes del Norte de Lanzarote
y Riscos de Famara
Isla de Montaña Clara
Isla Graciosa · El Río
ATLANTIC
OCEAN · Haría
Lanzarote
Tinajo · Teguise
Parque Nacional San Bartolomé · Costa Teguise
de Timanfaya Tías·
Yaiza· **ARRECIFE**
Puerto
del Carmen
Playa Blanca

DON'T MISS

*** Teguise's Sunday market:** at the ancient capital.
*** Fundación César Manrique:** see a remarkable house built into a series of volcanic bubbles.
*** Jardín de Cactus:** Manrique's garden of cacti at Guatiza with over 1400 species.
*** Museo Agrícola El Patio:** prize-winning museum of country life.
**** Castillo de Santa Bárbara:** visit the castle perched on the lip of a volcanic crater. Now a museum.

Opposite: *The Jardín de Cactus, Manrique's imaginative use of an old quarry.*

Central Lanzarote

TEGUISE

Teguise was the ancient capital of Lanzarote from the days of Maciot de Béthencourt up until 1852, when the administration was transferred to Arrecife. Teguise was, in fact, named after Béthencourt's wife, who was the daughter of Guardafía, the last of the Guanche leaders. Founded in 1418, Teguise was often referred to as the *Villa Real* (the royal city), a term still used by many *Lanzaroteños*, who dismiss Arrecife as *El Puerto* (the port). The Béthencourt dynasty was followed by the Los Herreras family and then, between the 16th and

18th centuries, Teguise developed as a fine colonial town with some impressive churches, convents and domestic architecture. However, during these times there was always the danger of being raided by Berber pirates. The small alleyway at the side of the parish church is known as the **Callejon de la Sangre** (the alley of blood) after large numbers of women and children were slaughtered here in a raid in 1586. After Arrecife became the capital of Lanzarote, the glory of Teguise faded somewhat, but during the 1980s a restoration programme was undertaken, with the encouragement of César Manrique.

Below: *Teguise's distinctive parish church, Iglesia de San Miguel, overlooks the Plaza de la Constitución.*

Plaza de San Miguel

Nowadays, the charm of Teguise lies in its quiet and dignified streets. At the centre of things is the **Plaza de San Miguel** (officially called the Plaza de la Constitución), with its fountain and Norfolk Island pines guarded by two imposing stone lions. Dominating the square is the parish church, the **Iglesia de San Miguel**, also known as the Iglesia de Nuestra Señora de Guadalupe. It has a bell tower of brown volcanic rock capped with a white octagonal belfry. The rest

Opposite: *The ancient capital of Teguise seen from the rim of the volcano Guanapay.*

CLIMATE

Located between the windier, wetter north and the sunnier, arid south, central Lanzarote can be said to have the average climate of the island. In January the mean temperatures are 17°C (63°F) with 50mm (2in) of rain, but by July, temperatures have risen to 25°C (77°F) and rainfall is rare.

of the exterior is white with dark stone corners. Do admire the stone doorway on the south side. The church was damaged by pirates on numerous occasions and suffered a further blow in the early 20th century when it was ravaged by fire, leading to extensive renovation. The interior is light with much white plasterwork. Note the pillars of dark volcanic stone, the rounded arches and the painted ceiling. Remember that the church, together with most of the other monuments in Teguise, closes in the afternoons.

On the south side of Plaza de San Miguel, there is a small building known as **La Cilla**. It was once a tithe barn, where the payments were collected from the local farmers and paid to the Bishop of Gran Canaria. Today La Cilla is occupied by a branch of the Caja de Canarios savings bank. On the west side of the plaza is the **Palacio Spínola**. More a town house than a palace, it was built in the mid-18th century and made from blocks of lava and timber supports. After being occupied by various noble families, it came into the hands of the Río Tinto company, who agreed to restore it. The *palacio* was then bought by the town council in 1984 and converted into a museum. In 1989 it was made the official residence of the Governor of the Canary Islands when he or she is in Lanzarote. All the rooms are open to the public and include living rooms, the bathroom, the kitchen and the courtyard. The Palacio Spínola is open from

Monday to Friday (with the exception of Wednesdays) between 09:00 and 15:00, and on Saturdays and Sundays between 09:30 and 14:00; tel: 928 845181. It also houses occasional art exhibitions.

Convents

Teguise has two important convents, one being the **Convento de San Francisco**, which was built by Franciscan missionaries in the late 16th century, although the convent's church is all that remains today. The exterior has some fine stonework including an unusual spiral pattern over the main door. The interior has two naves, one larger than the other, and the decoration is mainly *Mudéjar* in style. The most attractive features are the three altarpieces, a carved wooden pulpit, and a font made of volcanic stone. The Convent of San Francisco is open from Monday to Friday between 10:00 and 16:00 (except Tuesdays), and on Saturdays and Sundays between 10:00 and 15:00. The **Convent of Santo Domingo** can be found in the southwest of Teguise and is believed to have been founded in 1726. Renovations began in the 1980s, but were abruptly

WOODEN BALCONIES

There is a long tradition of woodcarving in the Canary Islands, both in craftwork and in the Plateresque style of carving found in church interiors dating from the 16th and 17th centuries. The wetter, western Canary Islands have plenty of Canary pine available, and inevitably the detailed carving style spread into domestic architecture. The pine is easily carved, but also very durable and best seen in the intricate balconies of fine mansions. Lanzarote, unfortunately, with its arid climate, does not have any Canary pine trees, so all the timber had to be imported. Ornate balconies, therefore, were mainly confined to the wealthy townhouses and *palacios* of Teguise, where they were status symbols.

Above: *The busy Sunday market in Teguise attracts tourists from all over the island.*

---

halted when over 100 partly mummified skeletons (possibly of Guanche origin) were found in the crypt.

Domestic Buildings

Teguise has a number of domestic buildings of note. **Casa Torres** dates from the 18th century. **Palacio Herrera-Rojas** once housed the island's archives, but they were destroyed by Berber pirates, and it now has an art gallery. **Casa Parroquial** was a barracks in the 17th century, while **Casa Cuartel** was once a prison. The architecture of the domestic buildings is typified by corners of black or red volcanic stone, with whitewashed walls and varnished wooden doors and windows. The occasional balcony and traditional chimney can also be seen. Another interesting part of Teguise can be found at the back of the parish church. This is the **Parque la Mareta**, which was once the location of a large reservoir, from where water was piped all over the island.

Sunday Market ***

Teguise's peace and quiet is interrupted on Sundays, when a lively market is held in Plaza San Miguel and the surrounding streets and alleyways. This is a popular excursion for visitors from the resorts in the south of the island. There are many stalls selling craft items, jewellery, ceramics, goats' cheese and other local specialities. Folklore performances often take place and the local restaurants do a roaring trade. The market runs between 09:00 and 14:00. There are also numerous shops and galleries in Teguise selling quality items including the *timple*, a traditional Canarian stringed instrument which is made in the town. Be prepared for chilly winds during the winter months.

EXHIBITION ROOMS
1. From the Canaries to America
2. The Castle
3. The Canary Way of Life
4. The Journey
5. The Memories of an Emigrant
6. The Emigrant's Luggage
7. Personal Illustrations
8. Conference Room

Crater of Volcano Guanapay

KEY
Crater
Path

Not to Scale

Castillo de Santa Bárbara

Castillo de Santa Bárbara **

In the east, looming over Teguise, is the extinct volcano **Guanapay**, which rises to 425m (1394ft), some 135m (443ft) above the town. Perched right on the rim of the crater of the volcano is the **Castillo de Santa Bárbara**. The original structure was a watchtower built in the early 16th century by Sancho de Herrera and used to look out for pirates coming inland from the east coast. After the bloodthirsty invasion by the Berber pirate Morato Arráez in 1586, King Felipe II sent the master fortress builder **Leonardo Torriani** to strengthen the fort. Within ten years the castle was looking very much as it does today.

Below: *Built in the late 16th century by Torriani, Castillo de Santa Bárbara is perched on the rim of a volcanic crater.*

COCHINEAL

The production of cochineal is one of Lanzarote's more unusual industries. Cochineal is a red dye made from the larvae of the cochineal beetle (*Cocus cacti*). The production is centred around the villages of **Guatiza** and **Mala** in the east of the island. Here you can see scores of fields growing the **prickly pear** (*Opuntia ficus-indica*) on which the cochineal beetle feeds. The beetles' larvae are collected and killed in hot water. They are then dried in the sun and crushed, resulting in a powder that forms the red dye. The industry suffered when synthetic dyes were introduced in the late 19th century, but today, with the emphasis on natural products, cochineal farming is making a comeback. Cochineal is used to colour soft drinks and it is also used in cosmetics, foods and pharmaceuticals. It is even said to provide the red colour in Campari!

By the 20th century it had become rather decrepit and in 1989 the local council took responsibility for its renovation. Since 1991 the castle has housed the **Museo del Emigrante**. Over the last 300 years, periods of drought and famine have forced many *Lanzaroteños* to emigrate to Latin America, particularly to Cuba and Venezuela. The museum traces their hardships with documents, prints, letters, boarding cards, passports and maps, along with artefacts and possessions such as luggage, typewriters, sewing machines and clothing. There are also models of the types of sailing and steam ships that transported the emigrants. The museum is open from Tuesday to Friday between 10:00 and 16:00, and on Saturdays and Sundays between 10:00 and 14:00. There is a good road from Teguise to the castle, with a small car park next to the entrance. It is possible to walk to the castle, but this is not advisable in hot weather. A rough track runs around the crater's rim and many visitors walk down into the bottom of the crater, as is shown by the number of names formed with stones.

COSTA TEGUISE AND THE EAST COAST

There are three main resorts on Lanzarote – Playa Blanca, **Costa Teguise** and Puerto del Carmen. Of these, Costa Teguise is the newest and smartest and has the distinction of having been built entirely from scratch on land that was formerly lava fields and salt pans. The work began in the late 1970s, spurred on by the opening of the luxury **Meliá Salinas Hotel**. With its central atrium, water gardens, three courtyards of restaurants and plethora of tropical plants, it was a sensation when it opened and it remains Lanzarote's top hotel today. However, further developments in Costa Teguise were not so smooth. César Manrique had played a part in its initial planning, with the Canary-style fishing village of **Puerto Marinero** surrounded by traditional buildings. However, tourists were slow to come and the development firm went bankrupt. Construction was taken over by a company from the Spanish mainland, who relieved Manrique of his consultancy and proceeded to develop the resort in a way that many people feel is not in harmony with the original concept.

Today, Costa Teguise is still growing and will eventually be able to offer 40,000 beds for tourists. A further three hotels have been built, as well as scores of apartment blocks and villas. There are a number of commercial centres, where most of the shops, restaurants and entertainment can be found. Costa Teguise has five **beaches** of white sand. The largest of these is **Playa de**

Opposite: *The Meliá Salinas, Lanzarote's top hotel, is located at the resort of Costa Teguise.*

Right: *One of the 10,000 cacti in Manrique's Jardín de Cactus.*

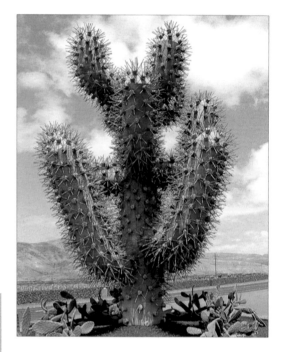

las Cucharas, which offers a full range of water sports.
Playa de los Charcos is protected by sea walls and is the
location of the Lanzarote Beach Club.

Costa Teguise has proved to be popular with people
wishing to buy homes on Lanzarote, including royalty
and a number of celebrities. Although the future of the
resort is assured, potential visitors should remember that
the site covers some 11km² (4.2 square miles) and many
parts have a rather sterile, unfinished look. Many
tourists at Costa Teguise find that a hired car is helpful
to reach the various facilities at the resort.

Costa Teguise is the location of the only golf course
on Lanzarote, situated just northwest of the resort.
Designed by John Harris, it is an 18-hole (par 72) course,
with a shop, driving range, bar and restaurant. With
over 3000 palm trees, the lush course contrasts strangely
with the barren volcanoes and lava fields around it.

Acua Lanza Water Park *

Right next to the golf course is the **Acua Lanza Water Park**, which offers a full range of slides and pools, providing an ideal day out for families. The water park is open daily between 10:00 and 18:00. Buses, free of charge, pick people up from various parts of the island.

Guatiza Region

From Costa Teguise the coastal road leads northwards and eventually reaches the towns of **Guatiza** and **Mala**, the centre of the cochineal-producing industry. Here are fields of the prickly pear cactus on which the cochineal insect feeds. If you look closely at the cacti you may see the silver-grey marks left by the beetle. Guatiza is a prosperous-looking town, with a main street lined with mature eucalyptus trees – an unusual sight in Lanzarote.

Jardín de Cactus ***

Just north of Guatiza on the right-hand side of the road is one of the island's main attractions – César Manrique's **Cactus Garden**. It is located in an old *rofero* (quarry), where local farmers dug out volcanic lapilli (*see* panel, page 101) for their fields. The garden has nearly 10,000 cacti of 1420 species brought from all over the world, but the most remarkable one is the metal sculpture by Manrique, 8m

Below: *There is no mistaking which toilet to enter at the Jardín de Cactus.*

WINDMILLS AND OTHER FORMS OF ENERGY

Lanzarote has no deposits of fossil fuels such as coal, oil or natural gas. Nor can it generate electricity by using running water, owing to low precipitation levels. The rainfall is also insufficient to construct reservoirs, so desalinization plants have been built to supply drinking water. Inevitably, there has been research into renewable forms of energy. Fortunately, Lanzarote has plenty of sun and wind and it is now standard for new houses and industrial premises to have solar power. Windmills have always been used on the island to grind grain, and now the first modern wind farm has been built on the hills near Los Valles to generate electricity. Others are likely to follow.

(26ft) in height, just outside the main entrance. Dominating the garden is a restored windmill, which shows clearly the way corn was ground to make *gofio*. There is also a small shop, a classy Manrique-designed restaurant, and a number of Manrique's paintings are on show in the entrance area. Don't miss the toilets with their extraordinary and amusing symbols for men and women.

A minor road leads from Guatiza through the cactus fields to the small coastal village of **Los Cocoteros** where some development has recently occurred. There are a few abandoned salt pans here that attract wading birds during the migration season.

Los Valles

Inland from Guatiza, along the GC700 route, is the attractive village of **Los Valles**. Its full name is Los Valles de Santa Catalina, as its original residents resettled here from the village of Santa Catalina in 1730 when their homes were buried under lava from the Timanfaya eruptions. The new inhabitants have worked hard to make their adopted area productive, and the valley-side terraces have crops of beans, potatoes and barley. This is one of the best spots on the island to see people working the fields in the traditional way with the time-honoured headwear and donkeys and camels (often harnessed together) pulling farm equipment. Los Valles is also a good place to note how, in rural farming communities, the *Lanzaroteños* add new blocks and extensions to their houses when their sons and daughters get married. It is worth taking a detour northwards from Los Valles to the **Ermita de las Nieves**, a small whitewashed chapel located at 643m (2110ft) above sea level. From this quiet and windy place there are wonderful views of the Risco de Famara cliffs and the sandy plain of El Jable. Just northeast of Los Valles is the **Parque Eólico** wind farm. The public are not allowed on the premises, but it offers an excellent photo opportunity.

Fundación César Manrique ★★★

Take the L210 road north out of Arrecife towards **Tahiche**. After a short distance there is a distinctive Manrique wind chime sculpture on a roundabout. Turn left here and just to the right is the **César Manrique Foundation**, located in the house that the artist occupied from 1968 to 1987, after which he moved to a farmhouse in Haría. In 1992 his former house became the headquarters of the César Manrique Foundation and was opened as a museum. The ground floor looks like a standard example of Canarian architecture, but Manrique had always wanted to live with the lava, and the house is built over five lava 'bubbles' dating from the volcanic eruptions that took place between 1730 and 1736. The bubbles are linked by tunnels, and throughout there is the striking contrast between the blue-black lava and the

Above: *The entrance to the Fundación César Manrique is lush with bougainvilleas.*
Opposite: *Wind turbines provide a useful source of energy, as Lanzarote has no fossil fuels.*

Above: *A tasteful water feature at the César Manrique Foundation.*

whitewashed walls. Each of the bubbles was a separate room in the house and each was emphasized with a different colour scheme. Some are open to the sky, such as the dining room with its traditional stove. Water also plays an integral part in the design, with the pool and a tinkling fountain. In one bubble, a palm tree grows up through the roof of the lava. Back in the entrance area, at ground level, there is an art gallery which includes works by Picasso, Tapies, Miró and, of course, Manrique himself. The gallery has a huge picture window looking out over the lava fields, while outside there is a snack bar, a bookshop and a massive outdoor mural.

Few fail to be impressed by the César Manrique Foundation, and most visitors will feel the urge to see more of his imaginative projects. In fact, just 7km (4 miles) to the west is the **Monumento al Campesino**, a white cubist monument, some 15m (49ft) high, made from the remnants of old fishing boats and water tanks. The full name of the monument is *El Monumento Fecundidad al Campesino Lanzaroteño* (the Fertility Monument to the *Lanzaroteño* Peasant), and Manrique dedicated the sculpture to the forgotten endeavours of the unknown farmers of Lanzarote. Look hard at the

monument and with some imagination you will be able
to pick out a farmer with his donkey and camel. Next to
the monument is the **Casa Museo del Campesino**, a
museum based on a traditional farmhouse. Here you can
see the farm equipment and tools, such as ploughs and
saddlery. Potters and basket-weavers display their traditional skills, while a dromedary works a mill to make the
gofio that is served in the museum's restaurant along
with other Canarian specialities. The museum is open
daily between 10:00 and 18:00.

San Bartolomé

Just to the south of the Monumento al Campesino, 7km
(4.3 miles) northwest of Arrecife, is the busy administrative town of **San Bartolomé**. In the central square is the
parish church, the town hall and a refurbished municipal
theatre. In Calle Constitución there is an **Ethnographic
Museum**, located in a traditional 18th-century house that
belonged to the Perdomo family. It has a comprehensive
collection of farming equipment, household items and
musical instruments showing how the island's culture
has changed over the last 200 years. The museum is open
from Monday to Friday (10:00–17:00) and on Saturdays

> ### THE CANARY PALM
>
> Because of its arid climate,
> Lanzarote is largely treeless.
> An exception, however, is
> the **Canary palm** (*Phoenix
> canariensis*), which is found
> in some numbers in the Haría
> area and parts of central
> Lanzarote, where its is often
> planted to provide shade
> around farmhouses. It is
> actually a very useful tree,
> as the leaves are an essential
> raw material for the handi-
> craft industry in the Canary
> Islands and they are used
> to make mats and baskets.
> Furthermore, the timber can
> be utilized for construction
> and the sap can be extracted
> to make palm honey.
> Unfortunately, in Lanzarote,
> the palm tree is far too
> valuable to chop down.
> Interestingly, the number of
> palms on the island is actually
> increasing as they are often
> planted in hotel gardens,
> where they make attractive
> landscape features.

Left: *Manrique's
Monumento al Campesino,
made from old boats and
water tanks.*

(10:00–15:00). A more modern attraction is **Eurokart**, Lanzarote's Go-Karting track, which is located just to the south of San Bartolomé on the Arrecife road. It is open from 10:00 until sunset and there is a bar and a childrens' playground; tel: 928 512195.

TIAGUA

North of the Monumento al Campesino roundabout the L220 road passes through **Mozaga** and then arrives at **Tiagua**, where, at the crossroads, you will find the simple, but delightfully photogenic, 18th-century **Ermita de la Virgen de Perpetuo**.

Museo Agrícola El Patio ★★★

Turn right at the crossroads and head in the direction of the windmills marking the location of the **Museo Agrícola El Patio**. Most visitors are enthralled by this agricultural museum, which well deserves the prizes it has won. The main building is a manor house, which once belonged to the Count de la Quinta. In the early 20th century, this was the largest and most efficiently farmed estate in Lanzarote, employing 25 farm workers and 20 camels. By the second half of the century, with the onset of tourism, many workers had left the land and taken up other work. In 1994 the estate was converted

Right: *Museo Agrícola El Patio shows how farming operated in the early 20th century.*

into a museum, which has already won a tourism prize. There are actually two museums here, based on either side of a large courtyard. On the right as you enter is the old manor house, which has been retained much as it was in the early 20th century. It is possible to wander through the rooms of the house – including living rooms, bedrooms and kitchen – and out into the grape press, bodega and grain store. There is also a meeting room, small chapel, wine museum and cactus garden. There are a variety of farm animals in the courtyard, including chickens, donkeys and a dromedary. The left-hand side of the courtyard is dominated by two restored windmills. One is the thin type made of wood, known as the female windmill, while the other is the larger plastered type with a tiled roof, known as the male windmill. It is possible to go inside both windmills and see the way in which corn was ground into *gofio*. There is also an example of an animal-driven mill. The buildings on this side of the courtyard form the main agricultural museum, with a wide collection of farming implements, harnesses and other artefacts. The tour ends at the bodega, where the local *El Patio* wine can be tasted, along with other delicacies such as goats' cheese. The Museo Agrícola El Patio is

Above: *The simple Ermita de la Virgen de Perpetuo at the Tiagua crossroads.*

Above: *Mancha Blanca's church, the Ermita de los Dolores, was threatened by encroaching lava in 1824.*
Below: *Nuestra Señora de los Volcanes at her place of honour in Mancha Blanca's church.*

open from Monday to Friday (10:00–17:30) and Saturdays (10:00-14:30), tel: 928 529134, www.museoelpatio.com

TINAJO REGION

From Tiagua the L220 swings northwest towards a conglomeration of prosperous agricultural villages. **Tinajo** is the main administrative village of the north and it is famous for the skill of its wrestlers – look out for the arena on the road to the south of the village. The parish church of San Roque, which has a sundial dated 1881 on its roof, is also worth a look. The interior has an impressive wooden *Mudéjar* ceiling and some fine statues, including one by Luján Pérez, the best-known Canarian sculptor. Linked with Tinajo, to the south, is the village of **Mancha Blanca**, famous for its church, the **Ermita de los Dolores**, and its statue, Nuestra Señora de los Volcanes. The church was built in honour of the virgin, who, it is claimed, saved the village from destruction in 1824 when the nearby volcano of Tinguatón erupted. The island's main fiesta and pilgrimage takes place here every September.

Northeast of Tinajo and south of the village of **Sóo** is the sandy plain of **El Jable**. This area is well known to bird-watchers as it is the best spot on the island to see Lanzarote's desert species, such as houbara bustard, stone curlew, cream-coloured courser and trumpeter bullfinch.

THE NORTH COAST

Generally rocky and inhospitable, the north coast has few settlements, with the notable exception of **La Santa**, a growing village sustained by the large sporting complex of **Club La Santa**. The club is able to offer facilities for 64 Olympic sports, a fact confirmed in the *Guinness Book of Records*. Professional international sportspeople flock here in the winter for warm-weather training, but there are many courses available for amateurs and families. The club has an Olympic-sized swimming pool, an athletics stadium and an artificial lagoon specially created for beginners' courses in windsurfing. La Santa village benefits from the proximity of the club and has a number of thriving fish restaurants. Just to the west of the club is a low-lying peninsula known as La Isleta, which was formerly an island. A road runs all the way around **La Isleta**, providing excellent points to watch surfers and sailboarders.

Further along the coast is the only other settlement, the pretty fishing village of **La Caleta de Famara**, where César Manrique spent his childhood. There are one or two good seafood restaurants in the village. This marks the start of Lanzarote's best sandy beach, the **Playa de Famara**. Unfortunately it is plagued by strong winds and tides and is usually too dangerous for swimming. A shipwreck confirms the strength of the Famara winds. The *playa* is backed by huge cliffs called the **Risco de Famara**, which rise to over 600m (1969ft) and are a popular location for hang-gliding.

Below: *Windsurfing is one of many activities provided at the La Santa Sports Centre.*

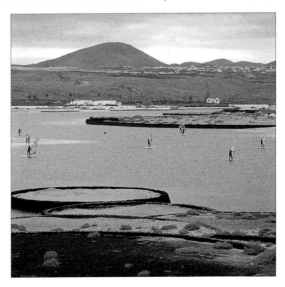

Central Lanzarote at a Glance

BEST TIMES TO VISIT

Central Lanzarote can be visited at any time of the year, but be prepared for strong winds on the north coast in the winter. In summer, the inland areas can be hot. The fiesta at Mancha Blanca, in September each year, celebrates the Virgin of the Volcanoes. It should not be missed.

GETTING THERE

Buses run from Arrecife to most of the villages of central Lanzarote, but the service is patchy. There are few links with the main resorts. **Coach** excursions only visit the main tourist locations. A hired **car** is the most convenient way to reach central Lanzarote.

GETTING AROUND

Once again, a hired **car** is essential to cover the best locations in the area. It is also the most convenient way to explore this region, as sign-posting and road surfaces are usually excellent and the distances involved are small. There is also a very good network of petrol stations.

WHERE TO STAY

There is little, if any, accommodation available in central Lanzarote, except in the resort of Costa Teguise. Even here there is no accommodation in the budget range. Beds in the self-catering apartments far outnumber those in hotels.

Costa Teguise
LUXURY
Hotel Meliá Salinas, Avda Islas Canarias s/n, Costa Teguise, tel: 928 590040, fax: 928 590390. Beachfront hotel with superb atrium, numerous restaurants, high-class rooms and sub-tropical gardens.

MID-RANGE
Hotel Teguise Playa, Avda del Jablillo s/n, Costa Teguise, tel: 928 590654, fax: 928 590979. High-standard hotel overlooking Playa del Jablillo, with leafy atrium and free-form pools.
Hotel Oasis, Avda del Mar s/n, Costa Teguise, tel: 928 590410, fax 928 590791. Modern hotel next to Playa del Ancla. Excellent leisure facilities.
Lanzarote Gardens, Avda Islas Canarias 13, Costa Teguise, tel: 928 590100, fax: 928 591784. Good family aparthotel near to Las Cucharas beach.
Celeste, Avda Islas Canarias s/n, Costa Teguise, tel: 928 591720, fax: 928 592482. Centrally located apartments, close to windsurfing school.
Tahiche, Plaza Montaña Clara, Costa Teguise, tel: 928 590118, fax: 928 590117. Family-friendly, self-catering apartments.
Los Zocos, Avenida Islas Canarias, Costa Teguise, tel: 928 592122, fax: 928 592528. Self-catering apartments with a buffet restaurant, close to beach.
Sirocco, Avda Islas Canarias s/n, Costa Teguise, tel: 928 592000, fax: 928 590242. Stylish apartments around a free-form pool.

WHERE TO EAT

For fresh seafood, head to La Santa and La Caleta on the north coast. A number of inland towns and villages, particularly in Teguise, serve traditional Canarian dishes. Costa Teguise has a variety of international food outlets.

Teguise
MID-RANGE
Acatife, Calle San Miguel 4, Teguise, tel: 928 845037. International food with a Canarian flavour in an atmospheric 18th-century house.
Ikarus, Plaza 18 de Julio, Teguise, tel: 928 845332. Fine food in an old manor house with its own art gallery. Open evenings only.
La Cantina, Calle León y Castillo 8, Teguise, tel: 928 845109. Spanish food and *tapas* in 18th-century *palacio*.

Costa Teguise
MID-RANGE
Mahatma, Avda de Jablillo, Costa Teguise, tel: 928 591967. One of the few genuine Indian restaurants.
El Pescador, Pueblo Marinero, Costa Teguise, tel: 928 590874. Interesting ambience in this harbourside restaurant.

Central Lanzarote at a Glance

La Graciosa, Hotel Meliá Salinas, Costa Teguise, tel: 928 590040. Pricey international food in the island's top hotel.

Meson El Establo, Avda de Teguise, Costa Teguise, tel: 928 816437. Specialist steakhouse, popular with golfers.

BUDGET

The commercial centres at Costa Teguise, such as Las Cucharas and Las Maretas, have a range of budget outlets such as Tex-Max, Chinese and American fast-food chains.

Chino Chu Lin, Calle Tandarena, Costa Teguise, tel: 928 592011. The best of a number of Chinese restaurants in the resort, with a takeaway service.

Guatiza

Jardín de Cactus, Guatiza, tel: 928 529397. After viewing Manrique's Cactus Garden, take a snack in the restaurant that he designed.

Mozaga

Casa Museo de Campesino, San Bartolomé, Mozaga road, near Monumento al Campesino, tel: 928 520136. Buffet-style museum restaurant serving traditional Lanzarote dishes. A good place to try *gofio*.

La Santa

MID-RANGE

La Santa, Tinajo Road, La Santa. Specializes in locally

caught fish. Popular with both locals and sporting types from Club La Santa.

La Caleta

El Risco, La Caleta, tel: 928 366397. Excellent seafood restaurant, with Manrique connections.

Casa Ramon, Calle Callejon, La Caleta. Simple fresh seafood and paella, with great views of the Risco de Famara cliffs.

TOURS AND EXCURSIONS

There are a number of travel agents in Costa Teguise who arrange excursions to venues throughout the island. The most popular attractions in the central Lanzarote area are the water park at Costa Teguise, the town of Teguise with its Sunday market, and the Museo Agrícola El Patio at Tiagua. Another popular excursion follows 'In the Footsteps of César Manrique', calling at the Cactus Garden at Guatiza, the Fundación César Manrique, and other attractions in the north of the island linked with the great *Lanzaroteño*.

USEFUL CONTACTS

Oficina de Turismo. There is just one tourist information office in the area – at Costa Teguise in Avda Islas Canarias (between the Lanzarote Beach Club and Hotel Meliá Salinas). It is open from 08:00–13:00, tel: 928 590810.

Windsurfing. There are two centres at Costa Teguise: Windsurfing Club, tel: 928 590731, and F2 Windsurfing Center, tel: 928 591974.

Diving at Costa Teguise: Calypso Diving, tel: 928 590879, and Diving Lanzarote, tel: 928 590407.

Internet Café. You can surf the net at Café Meral, Las Coronas, Avenida del Mar 24, Costa Teguise.

ENTERTAINMENT

There is little in the way of nightlife in central Lanzarote, apart from at Costa Teguise. Here, music bars include **Saxo**, while **Treble** is a lively sports bar. **Cariatico**, at the commercial centre, Las Maretas, is a popular nightclub.

SHOPPING

Most villages in central Lanzarote have shops selling local craft items, such as basketwork, embroidery, pottery and jewellery. The **César Manrique Foundation** has an outlet at La Lonja, Plaza 18 de Julio, Teguise. Don't miss the **Sunday market** in the centre of Teguise, where a number of stalls sell craft items. Many of the goods sold, however, are not Canarian craftware, but cheap items from abroad. Souvenirs can also be bought at the shops in the commercial centres at Costa Teguise, such as Las Maretas and Las Cucharas.

5
Southern Lanzarote and Timanfaya National Park

Southern Lanzarote, an area of contrasting features and extremely varied landscape, is dominated by the **Timanfaya National Park** containing over 30 volcanic cones within its boundary – this is every visitor's favourite excursion. These same volcanoes left vast areas of lava flows, with their dark jagged surfaces, which are known as *malpaís* or badlands. Despite the fact that they were formed over 250 years ago, these lava flows have little plant life because of Lanzarote's arid climate. South of the lava field lies the flat gravel plain of **El Rubicón**, which is almost totally devoid of vegetation. In contrast, fine crops of grapes are grown in volcanic granules called *picón* in the fertile valley of **La Geria**. The coastline is also varied; **Papagayo** in the south is typified by sandy beaches while in the north, at **Los Hervideros**, the Atlantic waves have etched out the lava cliffs into strange shapes and nearby, at **El Golfo**, the waves have eaten into the cone of a volcano, exposing layers of ash and lava, leaving a strange green lake in the crater floor.

SOUTHERN LANZAROTE

The south of the island is home to two of Lanzarote's main tourist resorts, but they are very different in character. Lively **Puerto del Carmen** stretches for 5km (3 miles) along the coast, with three magnificent beaches and all the trappings of a major resort. **Playa Blanca**, near the southern tip of the island, appeals to those who are looking for a quiet holiday. The south also has some attractive villages, with **Yaiza** often winning awards for

DON'T MISS

*** Timanfaya National Park:** the moon-like landscape of the 'Mountains of Fire' is a must for any visitor.
** El Golfo:** a volcanic crater eroded by the sea, leaving a bright green lagoon.
** Los Hervideros:** waves eroding the volcanic cliffs into cave arches and stacks.
** Beaches:** Lanzarote's best beaches are found in the south of the island.
** La Geria:** see vines grown in volcanic *picón*.
* Femés:** a village on a hill with stunning views.

Opposite: *El Diablo (the Devil) makes an apt logo for Timanfaya National Park.*

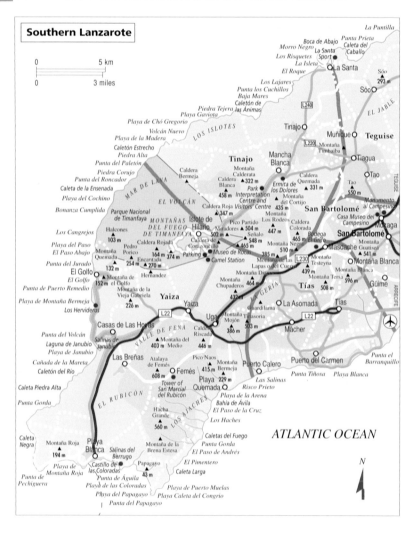

Southern Lanzarote

0   5 km

0   3 miles

La Puntilla
Boca de Abajo   Punta Prieta
Morro Negro   La Santa   Caleta del
Los Risquetes   Sport   Caballo
La Isleta
El Roque   La Santa
Sóo
293 m
Los Lajares   Sóo
Punta los Cuchillos
Baja Mares
Caletón de   EL JABLE
Piedra Tejera   las Ánimas
Playa Gaviota
Playa de Chó Gregorio
Volcán Nuevo   LOS ISLOTES   Tinajo   Muñique   Teguise
Playa de la Madera
Caletón Estrecho   Montaña
Piedra Alta   Mancha   Timbaiba   Tiagua
Punta del Paletón   Blanca
Piedra Corujo   Caldera   Tinajo   Montaña   Caldera   Tao
Punta del Roncador   Bermeja   Calderata   Quemada   550 m
Caleta de la Ensenada   Caldera   ▲322 m   Ermita de   ▲331 m
Playa del Cochino   Blanca   Park ● los Dolores   Monumento
458 m   Interpretation   Montaña   al Campesino
Bonanza Cumplida   EL VOLCÁN   Centre and   del Cortijo
Parque Nacional   Visitors' Centre   435 m   San Bartolomé   Casa Museo del
Los Cangrejos   de Timanfaya   MONTAÑAS Islote de   Caldera Roja   347 m   Montaña   Campesino   Mozaga
Halcones   DEL FUEGO Hilario   Pico Partido   Los Rodeos   Caldera
103 m   DE TIMANFAYA   ▲502 m Miradores ▲504 m   Colorada   San Bartolomé
Playa del Paso   Caldera Rojada   Señalo   447 m   Bodega
El Paso Abajo   Pedro   164 m 374 m   Caldera de   548 m   Montaña Negra   El Grifo   Masdache   Montaña
Punta del Jurado   Montaña   Porico   Parking ●   Corazoncillo   ▲465 m   510 m   L230   Montaña   ▲541 m
Quemada   254 m   ▲270 m   ● Museo de Roca   385 m   Montaña de las   Testeyna   Montaña Blanca
El Golfo   132 m   Encantada   ● Camel Station   Lapas o del Cuervo   439 m   Montaña Tersa
Punta de Puerto Remedio   Hernández   Montaña Diju   ▲   464 m   Tías   596 m   Güime
El Golfo   Montaña de la   Montaña   LAGERÍA   508 m
Playa de Montaña Bermeja   Vieja Gabriela   Yaiza   Chupaderos   ● La Asomada   Tías
Los Hervideros   226 m   Yaiza   433 m
Uga   Montaña Tasaoria   Guardilama
Casas de Las Horas   L22   Mojón   503 m   Mácher
Punta del Volcán   Salinas de   VALLE DE FENA   Caldera   386 m
Laguna de Janubio   Janubio   ▲403 m Medio   Riscada   446 m
Playa de Janubio   Las Breñas   Atalaya   Pico Naos   Montaña   Puerto Calero   Puerto del Carmen   Punta el
Cañada de la Mareta   de Femés   415 m   Bermeja   Barranquillo
Caletón del Río   608 m   ● Femés   Playa   229 m   Las Salinas   Punta Tiñosa   Playa Blanca
Caleta Piedra Alta   Tower of   Quemada   Risco Prieto
Punta Gorda   San Marcial   Playa de la Arena
del Rubicón   Bahía de Ávila
Caleta   EL RUBICÓN   Hacha   El Paso de la Cruz
Negra   Montaña Roja   Grande   Los Haches
194 m   Playa   560 m   Caletas del Fuego   ATLANTIC OCEAN
Blanca   Montaña de la   Punta Gorda
Playa de   Castillo de   Salinas del   Brena Estesa   El Paso de Andrés   N
Montaña Roja   las Coloradas   Berrugo   Papagayo   El Pimentero
Punta de   Punta de Águila   43 m   Caleta Larga
Pechiguera   Playa de las Coloradas   Playa de Puerto Muelas
Playa del Papagayo   Playa Caleta del Congrio
Punta del Papagayo

Opposite: *A variety of fun boats line the beach at Puerto del Carmen.*

its picture-postcard beauty. **El Golfo** is noted for its fish restaurants and its sunsets, while **Puerto Calero**'s photogenic harbour has the best collection of yachts on the island. Don't miss little **Femés**, perched high up in the mountains, providing the best views on Lanzarote.

Puerto del Carmen

Just ten minutes from Arrecife Airport in the municipality of Tías is Puerto del Carmen, Lanzarote's major resort, accommodating 60 per cent of the island's visitors and providing 30,000 beds in apartments and hotels. Puerto del Carmen stretches in a narrow ribbon along 5km (3 miles) of coast and includes three large sandy beaches. Despite its size, there are no high-rise structures and it is essentially a pleasant place to stay.

The Harbour

The old part of Puerto del Carmen is in the west and based around the old harbour. This was the original settlement, once known as **La Tiñosa**, a tiny fishing village. The harbour still has its fishing boats, now joined by a variety of other craft, such as diving boats, launches, ferries, fishing boats for deep-sea sports, and 'submarines' for underwater viewing. Next to the harbour is an adventure playground backed by a series of restaurants specializing in seafood.

East of the harbour, the picture changes. A long road, the **Avenida de las Playas**, forms a busy seaside strip. On one side is a promenade, rich in palms and colourful subtropical plants. The other side of the *avenida* consists of shops, restaurants, bars and amusement

TIMESHARE TOUTS

One of the irritations of a holiday in Puerto del Carmen is the ubiquitous timeshare tout, who hangs around the promenade and other crowded places. Officially known as an off-property contact, his job is to entice visitors, with ploys such as free gifts and holiday offers, to go to a timeshare location. Here, hard-sell techniques are employed. The idea is to persuade visitors to buy a share in a property in which they can take a holiday for one or two weeks a year for life. For some people the idea is attractive, but for many, especially those who like to visit a variety of holiday spots or enjoy staying in hotels, it is unsuitable. The best advice is to have a cooling-off period during which you can change your mind, and not to sign anything until you are absolutely sure of the financial implications.

Below: *Playa de los Pocillos, one of two popular beaches at the eastern end of Puerto del Carmen.*

arcades. It is said that there are over 200 restaurants in Puerto del Carmen and at least half of them are located along Avenida de las Playas. They include Indian, Chinese, Tex-Mex, Italian and just about every other type of cuisine you can imagine. Add to this list sports bars, English pubs, Irish bars and German beer gardens. Nightlife is around the various commercial centres, such as **Centro Atlántico**, with its nightclubs and discos. Further east the *avenida* becomes progressively quieter, with tasteful *urbanizaciónes* (housing estates), apartments and the occasional hotel.

Beaches **

Puerto del Carmen has three superb sandy beaches. The most westerly, and the busiest, is **Playa Grande** (also known, confusingly, as Playa Blanca – the same name given to the resort further south in the island). The town's tourist office can be found alongside the beach. Past the Punta el Barranquillo is the **Playa de los Pocillos**. Finally, at the eastern end of the town is the **Playa de Matagorda**. This beach is close to the airport and suffers from a degree of aircraft noise. All the beaches offer facilities, such as chair beds and sun shades, and there are a number of *chiringuitos* (beach

Puerto del Carmen

bars). The beaches are family-friendly and generally safe for swimming. Water sports are also available, such as windsurfing and water-skiing, while jet skis and pedaloes can be hired. An interesting feature of some of the town's beaches are the semicircular wind shelters made of stone, which are identical to the walls in the wine-growing areas in many parts of the island.

Inland Villages

Just 5km (3 miles) inland from Puerto del Carmen is the administrative centre of **Tías**. It is a sizeable village with nearly 11,000 inhabitants, making it the second-largest settlement on the island after Arrecife. However, there is little to interest the tourist, apart from the parish church of Nuestra Señora de la Candelaria, which has a curious double belfry. The church is the centre of the fiesta activities that take place in Tías every February. Further west is another administrative centre, **Yaiza**. Part of this village was destroyed by lava flows during the Timanfaya eruptions in the 18th century. Today, Yaiza is an attractive place with some expensive and dignified houses with flower-filled gardens. Palm trees line all the roads leading into the village, and the recent building of a bypass has increased the air of tranquillity in the settlement, which was a favourite of César Manrique. Head for the central square, which is the location of the parish church, the **Iglesia Nuestra Señora de Los Remedios**. Built in the late 17th century, it has been extensively restored in recent years. The interior has a painted wooden ceiling supported by black pillars of volcanic rock. There is also some fine carving on the gallery and

---

CLIMATE

The south of Lanzarote is the driest and sunniest part of the island. It also has less wind than the north. Average January temperatures are 18°C (64°F), rising in July to 25°C (77°F). Rainfall is low, and January and October are the wettest months. Be prepared for chilly winds during the winter months in Timanfaya National Park.

THE *ENARENADO* SYSTEM

The *enarenado* system of cultivation – using volcanic *picón* as soil and semicircular walls as shelters – is well known on Lanzarote. The system has been adapted in a number of ways for other uses, such as the growing of exotic shrubs on hotel grounds. More unusual are the semicircular stone walls used as wind shelters on some of the beaches in Puerto del Carmen, and at the golf driving range on former farmland just outside the resort, where golfers aim to hit golf balls into the stone walls and hollows of *picón*.

Above: *The dignified main square of Yaiza is backed by the 17th-century parish church.*

LANZAROTE WINES

All of the Canary Islands produce some wine, but the quality of Lanzarote's *vino* is the finest. Known as *malvasía*, it was well known to Shakespeare who referred to it as 'sack' or 'malmsey'. The *malvasía* grape was brought to Lanzarote from Crete and it produces a wine that is famous for its strength. Red (*tinto*), rosé (*rosado*), and sweet white (*moscatel*) are all produced here and can be bought in local supermarkets. Hotels always offer Lanzarote wines in their restaurants, although it is usually more expensive than the wine from the mainland.

---

altarpiece. Opposite the church is the **Benito Armas Cultural Centre**, named after the politician who lived here for over 60 years. Yaiza also has a number of craft shops and art galleries, the best known of which is the German-run **Galería Yaiza**.

On the opposite side of the bypass is Yaiza's sister village, **Uga**, which is located at the entrance of the valley of La Geria. Uga's main claim to fame is that it is the place where the camels which take tourists around the Timanfaya National Park are bred. The camels can often be seen walking along the path through the lava fields to the camel station.

Femés *

Until quite recently, the tiny village of Femés was one of Lanzarote's best-kept secrets. Nowadays it receives many visitors. It is perched on a col – at a height of 450m (1476ft) – in the mountain range known as **Los Ajaches**. It can be approached via Uga and this route passes through a fertile upland farming area. Look out for the house on the right-hand side with a garden full of remarkable objects, including a redundant military helicopter! In the centre of Femés is a charming little palm-lined square containing the whitewashed **Church of San Marcial del Rubicón**. The church was completed in 1733 (coincidentally when the Timanfaya eruptions were at their height) and was once the seat of a bishop. It replaced an earlier church that had been destroyed by pirates during the previous century. The interior of the church has a collection of model ships, but unfortunately the door is usually well and truly locked and only opened at the time of services. At the far end of the village square is a terrace known as the **Balcón de Femés**, providing superb views over the barren plain of **El Rubicón** and down towards Playa Blanca, with Fuerteventura in the distance. This is a great place to watch sunsets, particularly if you are having an evening meal at one of the two excellent restaurants in Femés. A clear hiking trail leads from the village to the summit of **Atalaya de Femés**, which rises to 608m (1995ft) and offers even more spectacular views. There is an alternative, steeper route down to Playa Blanca, via Las Breñas, which passes en route some *picón* quarries.

La Geria **

The L230 road runs northeast from **Uga** for 15km (9.3 miles) to **Masdache**, through a wine-producing area known as **La Geria**. It lies on the edge of the *malpaís* and is covered with black volcanic *picón*. Semicircular stone walls shelter vines from the drying northerly winds, and plants grow in the bottom of funnel-shaped hollows. The wine-producing area covers over 3000ha (7413 acres) and has become quite a popular tourist attraction. The *malvasía* wine that is produced here can be sampled at a number of bodegas. **Bodega La Geria**, which

---

DRY FARMING

On an island famed for its unusual landscapes, the most remarkable is found in the valley of La Geria. Here vines are grown by the ***enarenado*** method. They are planted in hollows, in the black granules of volcanic ash called *picón*, and sheltered by low semi-circular stone walls. The *picóns* act as hard sponges and store any rain that falls. They also trap any dew that collects, particularly on clear nights. The *Lanzaroteños* formerly used sand for this dry-farming process, but discovered – after the eruptions of the early 18th century – that *picón* was a far better water-holding material. So successful is the *enarenado* method that some vines can produce as many as 200kg (441lb) of grapes.

Below: *One of the largest bodegas in the wine producing valley of La Geria.*

also has a gift shop, is a favourite stop for coaches. **Bodega El Chupadero**, some 4km (2.5 miles) north of Uga, is just off the main road and you can sample wine more peacefully here. Further north, in Masdache, is **Bodega El Campesino**. On the outskirts of Masdache is the oldest of the bodegas, **El Grifo**, which was founded in 1775. It is generally accepted that this bodega makes the best wine on the island and it is available in all the top restaurants. El Grifo also has a small **wine museum**, which shows how wine-making equipment has changed over the years. The museum is open from Monday to Friday (10:00–18:00).

Coastal Erosion on the North Coast **

When the lava spread out from the volcanoes in the eruptions of the early 18th century, it not only covered villages and fertile farmland but also flowed into the sea, considerably increasing the land area of Lanzarote. Ever since then the Atlantic Ocean has been doing its best to claim the land back. At **El Golfo**, the sea has eroded away a volcano, exposing the wall of the crater and displaying a marvellous cross-section of lava and ash in a variety of colours. Beneath the crater wall is a half-moon-shaped lake called **Lago Verde** on account of its bright green colour that is caused by the micro-organisms, which are believed to be unique to this lake. Between the lake and the ocean is a beach of black volcanic pebble that is as good a place as any to search for specimens of

Right: *At Los Hervideros on the west coast, the waves of the Atlantic have eroded the lava flow into strange shapes.*

the green mineral called olivine. El Golfo can be approached from the south by a road leading to a small car park. Coach parties usually come from the north along a narrow path that leads to a viewing platform. This is close to the quiet village of El Golfo, which has a few fishing boats hauled up on the beach. There are half a dozen excellent fish restaurants here, many with terraces overlooking the sea and providing one of the best spots on the island to watch the sunset.

To the south of El Golfo, the road follows a dramatic stretch of coastline. To the left is Montaña Bermeja, a rusty red extinct volcano, while on the right, the sea crashes against the volcanic cliffs and seeks out the rocks' weaknesses in order to create stacks, arches and caves. The best place to view the action is at **Los Hervideros**, which literally means 'boiling waters'. From a convenient car park on the seaward side of the road, paths lead along the cliff top, giving viewing points to see the Atlantic waves crashing into the lava caves and arches. Choose a day when a heavy Atlantic swell is rolling in and you will be rewarded with the experience of pounding spray being sent metres into the air with a thunderous noise. Look out, too, for the bright red crabs that live on the rock faces in the spray zone above the waves.

Above: *The coastline near El Golfo, where rugged volcanic cliffs contrast with flat salt pans.*

COASTAL EROSION

Although the rock that forms volcanic cliffs is usually hard, it has many lines of weakness, such as faults and lava tubes, which can be attacked by the waves. The sheer **hydraulic force** of a wave can break open a rock face, but the shingle and sand contained in a breaking wave can wear away a rock face by **abrasion**. This results in the formation of **caves**, which later leads to erosive features such as **sea stacks** and **arches**. All of these examples can be seen in the **Los Hervideros** area in southwest Lanzarote.

Playa Blanca

A little further south, just past the edge of the *malpaís*, is a large salt-water lagoon, the **Laguna de Janubio**. On its landward side are the **Salinas de Janubio**, the only commercial saltworks still operating on the island, although in a much reduced capacity. At one time the salinas produced 350,000 tons of sea salt a year, but this is now down to about 10,000 tons, as refrigerators have replaced the need to use salt in order to preserve fish. The salt pans are laid out in a chequerboard pattern, with each pan having a slightly different colour, depending on the amount of water in it. The salinas are a good bird-watching location, particularly in the spring and autumn, when migrant waders find the habitat attractive. South of the salinas, two parallel roads cross the barren gravel plain of **El Rubicón** en route to the southern tip of the island and the resort of Playa Blanca.

Playa Blanca

Of Lanzarote's three main resorts, Playa Blanca is the smallest and most tranquil. Once a tiny fishing port, consisting of a few houses to the east of the harbour, it

FEEDING THE FISH

When looking down into the water of Lanzarote's harbours, visitors cannot help but notice the enormous number of fish swimming around. This contrasts strongly with the waters of the Mediterranean Sea, where fish are becoming very scarce due to over-fishing. It has become a popular pastime, in places such as Playa Blanca, to save unwanted bread and throw it to the fish. The water can literally surge with the feeding creatures!

has grown beyond recognition over the last 20 years, but still retains its charm. There is a small beach to the east of the harbour, but this is entirely inadequate considering the numbers that visit Playa Blanca. As a result, two new beaches have been constructed. To the east is the expansive and rather exposed **Playa Dorada**, still building up facilities such as shops and restaurants, but already offering a variety of water sports. To the west is the delightful little **Playa Flamingo**, sheltered by two moles and backed by subtropical gardens. This is a perfect family beach with very safe bathing. The three areas of Playa Blanca are linked by a promenade to the east of the harbour. The promenade is backed by shops and restaurants – many of which have terraces overlooking the sea. Just inland, and parallel to the waterfront, is another street of shops, pedestrianized in part and opening out onto a square to the east. Here we find the town's parish church.

Playa Blanca's harbour is a busy ferry port, with the Fred Olsen Line and Naviera Armas operating hourly car ferry services to Corralejo on the island of Fuerteventura, which can usually be seen clearly in the distance. Other craft in the harbour include game-fishing boats, 'submarines' for underwater viewing, diving-school craft and the *Marea Errota*, a two-masted sailing ketch known as the pirate ship.

> **DEEP-SEA FISHING**
>
> Visitors wishing to try their hand at deep-sea game fishing have plenty of opportunity in the south of Lanzarote. The marinas and harbours – at Puerto del Carmen, Puerto Calero and Playa Blanca – all have boats for hire, including all the necessary equipment, for small groups of anglers. The usual fish caught include marlin, swordfish, bonito and tuna. Some boats specialize in shark fishing. Book early to avoid disappointment.

Below: *A ferry leaves Playa Blanca harbour bound for Fuerteventura, which can be seen in the distance.*

NUDE SUNBATHING

Topless sunbathing in Lanzarote is common on beaches and around hotel and apartment pools. Full nudity, however, is offensive to *Canarios*. There are, nevertheless, beaches where nudity is tolerated. The best-known location in Lanzarote is the **Papagayo** beach area, just to the east of Playa Blanca. Before you rush to strip off though, remember to apply plenty of protection to those areas that do not normally see the sun!

Below: *An extinct volcano, Montaña Roja, forms a backdrop to the coastal promenade at Playa Blanca.*

There are plenty of walking options around Playa Blanca. Follow the promenade westwards and then take the paths that lead to the lighthouse, the **Faro de Pechiguera**, on the point of the same name. There are actually two lighthouses here – a low older structure and a tall new one. The more recent version was built at the prompting of César Manrique, who planned to have several of these around the shores of Lanzarote. However, the plan never came to fruition, presumably because it was too expensive.

A gentle walk eastwards along the promenade eventually leads to the **Castillo de las Coloradas**. It is believed that there was originally a small 15th-century castle on the same site, probably built by Jean de Béthencourt, but this was quickly destroyed by pirates. The present castle has a plaque dating its construction as 1769. It is possible to continue walking through building sites and rough tracks to the **Papagayo beaches**, although they are more easily reached by car or boat. Papagayo consists of a series of six beaches with pale gold sand, which are considered to be some of the best in the Canary Islands. They are popular with naturists, snorkellers and surfers. Since there is absolutely no shade and very few facilities on the Papagayo beaches, come prepared with your food, enough water and a sun-shade. A launch, *Cesar II*, runs at regular intervals between Playa Blanca and Papagayo. This makes a pleasant excursion, even if you do not wish to land at Papagayo.

However pleasant and charming Playa Blanca seems today, its charm may not last. At the time of writing, the resort was surrounded by building sites and a forest of construction cranes. Roads, street lighting and other services have already been laid out, and it is not too far-fetched to envisage Playa Blanca stretching from the Papagayo beaches in the east to the Pechiguera lighthouse in the west. Hopefully, the buildings will be tasteful, low-rise and in traditional Canarian style.

TIMANFAYA NATIONAL PARK

The Timanfaya area was declared one of Spain's eight national parks in 1974. Two of these are in the Canary Islands (the other is at Mount Teide in Tenerife). The park stretches from just north of Yaiza to Mazdache and westwards and covers a sizeable length of the northwest coast – an area of 52km² (20 square miles). Unlike most national parks in the world, Timanfaya is almost completely lacking in bird, animal and plant life. Instead, visitors see a barren, but colourful, volcanic landscape, as many would imagine the surface of the moon. The park gets its name from the village of

VOLCANIC MATERIAL

Lanzarote has a long history of volcanic eruptions and almost every type of rock found on the island is of volcanic origin. The hot liquid material within a volcano is called **magma**. When the volcano erupts the magma is thrown out and it can take a number of forms. The liquid material is known as **lava** and it can flow for long distances. Explosive activity creates **ash**, which can form thick layers, and some of the ash is coarse and known as **lapilli** or **picón**, which is quite common in Lanzarote.

Right: *Dromedaries transport visitors over the barren volcanic slopes in Timanfaya National Park.*
Opposite: *A road winds through the volcanoes in Timanfaya National Park; visitors to the park must stay in their vehicles.*

COLOURFUL VOLCANIC ROCKS

Many visitors to the Timanfaya National Park are fascinated by the variety of colours seen in volcanic rocks. Generally speaking, volcanic material becomes lighter with age, so that the more recent rocks of Lanzarote are still bright with colour. Most volcanic rocks owe their colours to their **mineral content**. **Copper** produces green and blue tints, while **iron** stains rocks brown and red. Many volcanoes in Lanzarote are named after their colours, such as **Montaña Roja** (red), near Playa Blanca, **Montaña Bermeja** (orange ochre), close to El Golfo, and **Montaña Negra** (black) at Masdache. A common pale green mineral found in the lava of Lanzarote is **olivine** (the gem variety is called **peridot**) and chunks of this mineral are sold in shops.

Timanfaya, one of ten settlements buried by lava and ash during the volcanic eruptions that occurred between 1730 and 1736.

Fortunately, we have an eyewitness account of the eruptions. Andrés Lorenzo Curbelo was the village priest at Yaiza at the time and he recorded the events in detail. He describes how the eruptions began in September 1730 and continued for six years. From 26 eruptions, lava and ash covered a large area of what was the most fertile farm land on the island, inundating villages and hamlets and flowing into the sea, which proceeded to boil. Curbelo describes how this resulted in thousands of dead fish species, many of which had never been seen before. Although 150km² (58 square miles) of land was devastated, nobody is believed to have died in the eruptions, as they managed to flee to the north of Lanzarote or to other Canary Islands.

Over 30 new volcanic cones were formed and large areas of black lava or coarse ash granules – known as lapilli or *picón* – were deposited as a result of the eruptions. These materials formed badlands or *malpaís*, and nearly 300 years after the eruptions they are still largely devoid of vegetation.

Visiting the Parque Nacional de Timanfaya ★★★

If holiday-makers have only time for one excursion while in Lanzarote, then it must be a trip to the Timanfaya National Park. Although most people take a coach excursion, it is possible to use a car, although this will involve transferring to one of the park's buses at some stage. Remember that roaming at will through the park is not allowed.

As you approach from Yaiza, the boundary of the park is marked by the 'fire-devil' sign at the side of the road. Shortly after this, on the left-hand side of the road, there is a car park marking the **camel station**. Here, over 100 dromedaries take visitors for a 20-minute ride over the volcanic slopes. Passengers sit in wooden seats on either side of the single hump, and it is important that the passengers are equally balanced, so the *camelleros* (dromedary handlers) use small sandbags to weigh down children or light adults. Hang on tight when the dromedary gets to its feet, as the seat will lurch forward. The camel station has a café, toilets and a small museum, the **Museo de Rocas**, which has numerous geological specimens from the park, along with information about the 'camels'. The museum is open from Monday to Friday (09:00–15:00).

A few kilometres further along the road an entrance fee has to be paid at a barrier. A road leads on for 2km (1.2 miles) to a hill known as the **Islote de Hilario**. *Islote* means an island of rock protruding above the surrounding lava, while Hilario is believed to have been a hermit who lived here for 50 years, accompanied only by his donkey. Crowning the hill is the **El Diablo Restaurant**, which was designed by César Manrique as a glass-walled circle and gives superb views over the volcanic

TYPES OF LAVA

When molten **magma** erupts from a volcano, the eventual form of the lava depends on a number of factors including its chemical composition and rate of cooling. The descriptive names that are given are often Hawaiian in origin, for its was in these islands that the first research was carried out. **Aa** (pronounced 'ah-ah') is viscous material that cools quickly and has a dark, clinker-like appearance. This is the most common type of lava on Lanzarote. **Pahoehoe** (pronounced 'per-hoyhoy') lava is glassier and lighter in colour and often cools as **ropey lava**. Some lava solidifies in the form of **pillows**, particularly after contact with water. **Basalt** is a fluid, black lava that travels for long distances and cools in hexagonal columns.

THE CAMEL

Most visitors to the Timanfaya National Park try their hand at riding a camel. But the beast that they are riding is actually a drome-dary. The **Bactrian Camel** (*Camelus bactrianus*) has two humps, while the camel seen in Lanzarote is the **Arabian Camel** (*Camelus dromedaries*) or **Dromedary**. Camels are large animals standing up to 2m (6.5ft) tall and their colours vary from brown, through fawn to almost white. Camels and drome-daries make excellent beasts of burden as they have large storage pockets for water in the stomach and food reserves in their humps. Their large, spreading, padded toes allow them to get a grip on soft loose ground. Lanzarote's dromedaries were originally imported from North Africa and today they still have Moroccan handlers or *camelleros*.

landscape westwards towards the sea. Much of the restaurant's food is grilled over a barbecue using natural heat from underground. The heat of the land below the surface is also demonstrated by the park's employees in a series of tricks; granules of hot *picón* are handed around (and very soon dropped), brushwood is placed in holes in the ground and then bursts into flames and, most spectacularly, water is poured into tubes set in the earth and erupts as steam, which shoots several metres into the sky like a man-made geyser. It is not surprising to learn that 6m (20ft) below the ground the temperature is 400°C (752°F)!

Visitors are now taken on a spectacular bus tour around the **Ruta de los Volcanes**, covering 10km (6.2 miles) and lasting about 40 minutes. The moon-like landscape is surprisingly colourful and it is possible to look down into craters, see dunes of *picón* and look into lava tubes. At one point the road passes through the steep walls of a collapsed tube. Unfortunately, although

Opposite: *Visitors are transported through the volcanoes of the Timanfaya National Park in the park's official bus.*

Right: *Lunch at El Diablo Restaurant is cooked using the residual heat of the volcano.*

stops are made, it is not possible to get out of the bus, so photographs have to be taken through the windows.

If by now you are hooked on vulcanology, then pay a visit to the park's **Visitors' Centre** (the Centro de Visitantes e Interpretación de Mancha Blanca). This is located a few kilometres north – on the outskirts of the village of Mancha Blanca. The building is on the left-hand side of the road and right in the middle of the lava fields. The museum was opened in 1996 and it is full of hi-tech equipment which demonstrates the working of volcanoes. Large windows look out onto the lava, with volcanoes in the background to give immediate and practical examples of the theory being explained. As well as geology, there are also displays of the natural and social history of Lanzarote. There are audiovisual demonstrations at regular intervals. Children enjoy the visit to the bowels of the centre where a simulated eruption may be experienced, complete with colour, noise and smoke!

The Visitors' Centre is also the only place where you can book guided hiking trips in the park. There are two walks on offer. One goes around the central volcanoes, while the other follows the northwest coast. Both are demanding – hikers should be fit and well equipped. The walks are very popular and usually fully booked several days in advance.

LONG-DISTANCE MIGRANTS

Butterflies are not particularly common in Lanzarote, largely owing to the lack of flowers and nectar on which they feed. However, two species that are often found in hotel grounds are the **monarch** (*Danaus plexippus*) and the **painted lady** (*Cynthia cardui*). While both species are resident and breed in the Canary Islands, they also undertake lengthy migrations northwards. The monarch is occasionally seen in the coastal parts of France and Holland, while the painted lady can often be seen in huge numbers all over northern Europe. In Britain, the painted lady can have two broods in favourable years, but it is unable to survive the northern European winters. Surprisingly, the monarch and the painted lady are often seen migrating northwards together.

Southern Lanzarote and Timanfaya National Park at a Glance

BEST TIMES TO VISIT

The south is the driest, sunniest and least windy part of Lanzarote, so it is a good place to be in winter. July and August can be hot, particularly if the sirocco wind is blowing. Be prepared for chilly winds if visiting the Timanfaya National Park in winter.

GETTING THERE

The south is easily reached from the rest of the island. There are regular bus services from Arrecife to the resorts of Puerto del Carmen and Playa Blanca, but not to the Timanfaya National Park.

GETTING AROUND

The bus service to the smaller towns and villages is patchy – a hired car is essential to reach the more remote locations. Roads and signposting are good, so navigating in the area is not a problem.

WHERE TO STAY

There are no *pensiónes* in the south of the island and therefore nothing in the way of budget accommodation. Almost all the accommodation in the south is confined to the resorts of Puerto del Carmen and Playa Blanca.

Puerto del Carmen
LUXURY
Hotel Los Fariones, Roque del Este 1, Puerto del Carmen, tel: 928 510175, fax: 928 510202. Dating from 1966, this traditional hotel is set in subtropical gardens and provides every comfort.
Hotel Jameos Playa, Playa de los Pocillos, Puerto del Carmen, tel: 928 511717, fax: 928 514219. Beachside hotel with excellent sports facilities.

MID-RANGE
Hotel La Geria, Playa de los Pocillos, Puerto del Carmen, tel: 928 510441, fax: 928 511919. Seafront hotel with good leisure facilities.
Hotel San Antonio, Avenida de las Playas 84, Puerto del Carmen, tel: 928 514200, fax: 928 513080. Older hotel with gardens and good facilities.
Apartamentos Playa Club, Avenida de las Playas 99, Puerto del Carmen, tel: 928 513719, fax: 928 510906. Apartments centrally located and well run.

Playa Blanca
LUXURY
Hotel Timanfaya Palace, Playa Blanca, tel: 928 517676, fax: 928 517035. Exclusive seafront hotel with impressive atrium and subtropical gardens.

MID-RANGE
Hotel Lanzarote Park, Urbanización Montaña Roja, Playa Blanca, tel: 928 517084, fax: 928 517348. Comfortable hotel with good leisure facilities right next to the beach.
Hotel Lanzarote Princess, Calle Maciot s/n, Playa Blanca, tel: 928 517108, fax: 928 517011. Large comfortable child-friendly hotel, set back from the town centre.
Sun Park Apartments, Playa Dorada, Playa Blanca, tel: 928 517021. Well-run apartments used by package tours. Close to Playa Dorada beach.

Yaiza
LUXURY
Hotel Rural Finca de las Salinas, Calle la Cuesta 17, Yaiza, tel: 928 830325, fax: 928 830329. Small, but luxurious country hotel in a converted 18th-century mansion, with a pool and its own vegetable garden.

WHERE TO EAT

The widest choice of restaurants to suit every taste and pocket can be found in Lanzarote's chief resort of Puerto del Carmen, where there are over 200 establishments. There is also a good selection in Playa Blanca, and some fine country restaurants serving traditional Canarian food in the inland villages of Uga, Yaiza and Femés. For the freshest seafood, head for the coastal village of El Golfo.

Puerto del Carmen
LUXURY
El Escuela de Fondeadero, Centro Cívico, Plaza del Varadero, Puerto del Carmen, tel: 928 511465. Immaculate Canarian food cooked by trainee chefs.

Southern Lanzarote and Timanfaya National Park at a Glance

MID-RANGE

La Fontaine, Calle Teide 9, Puerto del Carmen, tel: 928 514251. Close to the harbour, with a celebrated chef.

La Paella, Calle Matagorda, Puerto del Carmen, tel: 928 513460. As it name suggests, a variety of paellas are available, along with takeaways.

El Sardinero, Calle Nuestra Señora del Carmen 9, Puerto del Carmen, tel: 928 511933. Highly regarded seafood restaurant near the harbour.

El Varadero, Plaza del Varadero 34, Puerto del Carmen, tel: 928 825711. Traditional fish restaurant in an old boathouse. Good *tapas*.

BUDGET

Chu Lin, Calle La Penita, Puerto del Carmen, tel: 928 510223. One of the best of few Chinese restaurants with a takeaway service.

Playa Blanca
MID-RANGE

El Almacén de la Sal, Paseo Maritimo 12, Playa Blanca, tel: 928 517885. Popular restaurant in a converted salt store, with live music.

Brisa Marina, Paseo Maritimo 10, Playa Blanca, tel: 928 517006. Excellent seafood restaurant with a terrace overlooking the sea.

Casa Joaquín, Playa Flamingo, Playa Blanca, tel: 928 517438. Behind the beach at Playa Flamingo. International food and live music.

Yaiza
MID-RANGE

La Era, Calle El Barranco 3, Yaiza, tel: 928 830016. Local food and wine in a 300-year-old farmhouse converted by César Manrique, with delightful courtyards and gardens.

El Golfo

There are at least eight seafood restaurants in this hamlet.

MID-RANGE

El Hotelito, El Golfo, tel: 928 173272. Tiny hotel with excellent terrace restaurant.

El Golfo, tel: 928 173147. Excellent paella and other fish.

BUDGET

Other fish restaurants in El Golfo, most with sea views, include **Lago Verde**, **Plácido**, **Mar Azul** and **Casa Torano**.

Timanfaya National Park
LUXURY

El Diablo, Islote de Hilario, Parque Nacional de Timanfaya, tel: 928 840057. Superb restaurant, designed by Manrique, in the middle of the national park. Much of the food is cooked by volcanic heat. Open for lunch only.

Femés

There are two excellent restaurants in this tiny hill village:

MID-RANGE

Casa Emiliano, Femés, tel: 928 830223. Good local meat dishes, including rabbit.

Balcón de Femés, tel: 608 023093. Traditional Canarian dishes and international food. Marvellous views from the terrace.

TOURS AND EXCURSIONS

A full range of tours and excursions can be arranged from the resorts of Puerto del Carmen and Playa Blanca to all the main tourist attractions on the island. The three main excursions are to the **north of the island**, including the Mirador del Río, the Jameos del Agua and the Cueva de los Verdes. A popular trip around the **south of the island** visits the Timanfaya National Park, El Golfo and La Geria. Another well-patronized excursion is **In the Footsteps of César Manrique**. Some tour operators arrange day trips to the island of **Fuerteventura**, using the ferries from Playa Blanca. Local **boat trips** can be arranged from both Puerto del Carmen and Playa Blanca.

USEFUL CONTACTS

There are **Tourist Information Offices** in **Puerto del Carmen**, on the seafront, tel: 928 513351 (open from Monday to Friday 09:00–13:00 and 17:30–19:30, and on Saturday, 09:00–13:00), and at **Playa Blanca**, next to the ferry terminal, tel: 928 517794 (open from Monday to Friday 10:00–18:00).

6
A Day Trip to
Northern Fuerteventura

For many holiday-makers on Lanzarote, the idea of spending a day in the neighbouring island of Fuerteventura is an attractive possibility. It provides you with the opportunity of seeing another island in the Canaries, and you can decide whether it is suitable as a future holiday destination.

Getting to Fuerteventura is not a problem. Many travel companies run coach tours from Lanzarote to the northern part of Fuerteventura, and their excellent guides present an accurate flavour of the place. It is also possible to take hired cars on the ferries to Fuerteventura and, with four passengers in a car, some good deals can be negotiated. Two ferry companies operate the route from **Playa Blanca** in the south of Lanzarote to **Corralejo** in the north of Fuerteventura. Tickets can be purchased in the offices on the jetty at Playa Blanca. The **Fred Olsen** ferries leave Playa Blanca at 08:00, 10:00, 14:00, 16:00 and 18:00, returning from Corralejo at 09:00, 11:00, 15:00, 17:00 and 19:00 (website: www.fredolsen.es). The **Naviera Armas Line** ferries leave Playa Blanca at 07:00, 09:00, 11:00, 13:00 (not on Sundays), 17:00 and 19:00, returning from Corralejo at 08:00, 10:00, 12:00 (not on Sundays), 14:00, 18:00 and 20:00. Note that tickets are not interchangeable between the two lines.

DON'T MISS

*** Corralejo Dunes Natural Park: enjoy miles of empty beaches.
** Betancuria: visit the Cathedral of Santa María in the island's old capital.
* Isla de los Lobos: experience the peace and quiet just a boat ride from Corralejo.
* La Oliva: see fine 18th-century colonial houses.
* El Cotillo and Corralejo: try the superb seafood in these fishing settlements.

FACTS ABOUT FUERTEVENTURA
Fuerteventura is the second-largest of the Canary Islands, stretching approximately 100km (62 miles)

Opposite: *The Fred Olsen car ferry leaves Playa Blanca for the island of Fuerteventura.*

CLIMATE

Fuerteventura is the nearest of the Canary Islands to North Africa. As a result it is very arid, with rarely more than 150mm (6in) of **rain** annually, mostly falling during the winter months. **Winters** are warm, although the nights can be chilly. **Summers** are hot, particularly when the **sirocco** wind blows from Africa. Be prepared for strong **winds**.

from north to south, with a width of 40km (25 miles) at its maximum from east to west. It is the most sparsely populated of all the islands, with around 45,000 inhabitants. About 20,000 of these live in the capital, **Puerto del Rosario**. It is also the driest of the Canary Islands, with a mere 15cm (6in) of rain falling on roughly 24 days of the year. Fuerteventura's main products are fish, tomatoes and goats' cheese. Its chief foreign earner, however, is **tourism**, with some 1.2 million visitors a year. In the south of the island 90 per cent of the tourists are German, but the northern part of Fuerteventura is more popular with the British and Scandinavians, although many more nationalities enjoy visiting Fuerteventura.

Northern Fuerteventura

Historical Background

Fuerteventura was the second of the Canary Islands to be conquered by Europeans. The Norman **Jean de Béthencourt** and his ally **Gadifer de la Salle** landed on Fuerteventura in 1404, having previously conquered Lanzarote. They found between 6000 and 8000 Guanches, who on Fuerteventura were known as *Majoreros*, a word meaning 'cave-dwellers'. Spaniards later arrived in force, and the first cathedral was set up in 1426. However, the bishop resided on Gran Canaria – as did most of the landowners of the island.

For the next 300 years, Fuerteventura suffered from continuous raids by North African pirates, and it was not until the mid-19th century that it was felt safe to have the island's capital in a coastal location. The island government, **Cabildo Insular**, was set up in 1912. Then in 1927 it became part of the eastern province of the Canary Islands, along with Gran Canaria and Lanzarote.

Fuerteventura has always been politically conservative and gave considerable support to General Franco. In return, he did much to improve the infrastructure of the island. Tourism began to take off in Fuerteventura in 1966, and by the 80s and 90s tourist numbers were growing by 20 per cent a year.

Above: *Fuerteventura can be seen in the distance from Playa Blanca.*

ISLAND HOPPING

The independent traveller wanting to see more than one of the islands will have little problem getting around. There are regular domestic flights linking all the islands. The main airlines involved are Binter, Canarias Regional Air and Spanair. A cheaper, but slower, way of island hopping is by **boat**, with a choice of ferries, jet foils and hydrofoils. The main companies are Trasmediterránea, Lineas Fred Olsen and Naviera Armas. Corralejo in northern Fuerteventura is connected by two ferry services to Playa Blanca in Lanzarote. Puerto del Rosario is linked by ferry to the capital, Arrecife, and to Las Palmas in Gran Canaria.

Above: From a harbour-side café in Corralejo, Isla de los Lobos is visible in the distance.

A TOUR OF THE NORTH OF THE ISLAND

The following account describes a route that can be taken within a day. There is not enough time to visit all the places, so the choice depends on the visitor's interests.

Isla de los Lobos *

As you approach Fuerteventura, the volcanic island you see on the left is **Isla de los Lobos**, an island named after the wolf seals that once lived here. Sadly, the seals are long gone, having been killed off by fishermen years ago, but the local *cabildo* has tentative plans to reintroduce them here. It is possible to take a boat from Corralejo to Isla de los Lobos, where there is a tiny fishing village called **El Puertito**, with a small restaurant and some wonderful beaches. A track can be followed all the way around the island, passing the **lighthouse** at the northern tip. It is also possible to climb up to the crater of the extinct volcano **Montaña Lobos**, standing at 127m (416ft) high – the highest point on the island.

Corralejo *

From the ferry, **Corralejo** is seen to have a background of volcanic hills. However, unlike Lanzarote, it is over 7000 years since volcanic activity took place on Fuerteventura. Once a small fishing port, Corralejo is now a busy holiday resort, offering visitors some 15,000 beds. Although the town beach is rather small, there are miles of sand dunes to the south, where the main tourist developments are taking place. The harbour is busy, with car ferries running to Lanzarote and Las Palmas in Gran Canaria. Corralejo has a busy shopping centre, based around the main street, **Avenida Generalísimo Franco**, and the lively **Centro Atlántico**. There are good fish restaurants along the seafront and in **Plaza Felix Estavéz González**.

Parque Natural de las Dunas de Corralejo ✱✱✱

Leave Corralejo southwards on the FV1 road to Puerto del Rosario. On the left-hand side is the **Parque Natural de las Dunas de Corralejo**, an area of sand dunes that stretches for 7km (4.5 miles) along the coast. Here, two large multistorey hotels, **Tres Islas** and **Oliva Beach**, stand out like sore thumbs. They were built before the park was designated and no further construction allowed. The dunes are a popular haunt for naturists who are often in danger of getting sandblasted when the winds blow strongly in summer. This is also a great spot for surfing and sailboarding, with a number of shops in Corralejo selling all the required gear.

The end of the natural park is marked, on the landward side of the road, by the hulk of the volcanic cone of **Montaña Roja**, which rises to 312m (1023ft). Sand dunes are now replaced by *malpaís*. You then reach a Dutch development, **Urbanización Parque Holandes**, which has had a chequered history. Miles from anywhere and without the benefit of a decent beach, the resort was slow to take off and the original developers went bankrupt. Another firm has now taken over and construction has recommenced.

> ### TYPES OF DUNES
>
> Dunes are formed by the wind blowing grains of sand inland at low tide. There are three types of dunes. Initially they are **mobile** – the dunes are continually moving and are devoid of vegetation. Eventually they become **semi-fixed**, with sparse vegetation beginning to appear on them, mainly in the form of marram grass. Finally they become **fixed**, with movement ceasing and an almost total vegetation cover. The dunes at Corralejo, influenced by strong winds and aridity, are nearly all at the mobile stage.

Puerto del Rosario

The FV1 road now reaches **Puerto del Rosario**, which was made the capital of Fuerteventura as recently as 1860. Before that the administrative role was taken successively by Betancuria, Antigua and La Oliva – all sited inland and better protected from the raids of pirates. Prior to 1956 Puerto del Rosario was known as Puerto de Cabras (Goat Harbour), which was hardly a suit-

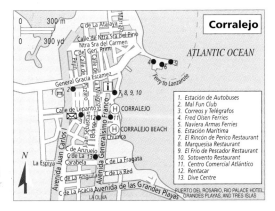

Corralejo

ATLANTIC OCEAN

Ferry to Lanzarote

1. Estación de Autobuses
2. Mal Fun Club
3. Correos y Telégrafos
4. Fred Olsen Ferries
5. Naviera Armas Ferries
6. Estación Marítima
7. El Rincón de Perico Restaurant
8. Marquesisa Restaurant
9. El Frio de Pescador Restaurant
10. Sotovento Restaurant
11. Centro Comercial Atlántico
12. Rentacar
13. Dive Centre

PUERTO DEL ROSARIO, RIO PALACE HOTEL, GRANDES PLAYAS, AND TRES ISLAS

NATURE'S MIRACLE PLANT

Fuerteventura's hard-pressed farmers have recently found that the island's climate is ideal for the production of the spiky, cactus-like plant known as **aloe vera** (*Aloe barbadensis miller*). Its healing properties were well known to the ancient Egyptians, who called it the plant of immortality, but it wasn't until the 1970s that it became popular in the health industry. The yellow juice in the plant is packed with antioxidant vitamins. It can be drunk like a fruit juice to relieve digestion problems, and applied to the skin as treatment for eczema and rheumatism. The more research that is carried out on aloe vera, the more benefits there seem to be and there are few, if any, side effects. Fuerteventura's farmers are, not surprisingly, increasing their production.

able name for the capital of the island. It began to develop as a port in the 19th century and continues to be the main industrial centre of Fuerteventura, with a number of industrial estates in the suburbs. It was also the home, for many years, of the **Spanish Foreign Legion**, who came here when Spanish Sahara gained its independence. The presence of so many soldiers fuelled the development of the red-light district of Barrio Chino, which is now being cleaned up.

Today, Puerto del Rosario has a population of 20,000 people, many of whom are immigrants from Andalucía and Galicia who work in the tourist and construction industries. Although it is the dominant settlement on the island, it makes few concessions to tourists. Even its main hotel, the **Hotel Fuerteventura**, a former *parador*, caters mainly for business people. The town beach, **Playa Blanca**, is used largely by locals.

Vistors on a one-day trip to Fuerteventura might wish to give Puerto del Rosario a miss, but it is a good shopping centre. The main shopping area runs from the **Plaza de España** on the promenade along **Avenida León y Castillo**. The only other item of interest in Puerto del Rosario is the **Casa Museo Unamuno**, based on the work of the Spanish poet and academic Miguel de Unamuno, who was exiled to Fuerteventura in the 1920s.

Opposite: *A restored windmill reminds visitors to the area that this was once a fertile valley.*
Right: *The valley that runs through the centre of Betancuria is dry for much of the year.*

HEADING INLAND

Take the FV20 road inland, and head towards Antigua. This route passes through the **Valley of the Windmills**. Up until the early 19th century this valley was fertile, and large amounts of wheat and maize were grown here – hence the windmills, which were used to grind the corn to make *gofio*. However, during the 1800s there was a prolonged period of drought, which caused the ground water to sink and become very salty. Many farmers emigrated to Latin America, and today the only agriculture in the valley is the production of aloe vera. Just outside **Antigua** a large restored windmill dominates the skyline. This marks a sort of museum village known as the **Centro de Artesanía el Molino de Antigua**. As well as the windmill, which still produces *gofio*, there is a restaurant serving typical Canary Island dishes, studios where craftsmen demonstrate their work, and a gift shop.

Antigua *

As its name suggests, Antigua is an ancient settlement. It was founded in 1485 and was briefly the capital of the island in the early 19th century, before handing over the role to La Oliva. Head for the main square and the parish church, the **Iglesia de Nuestra Señora de Antigua**. It dates from 1785 and has a fine *Mudéjar* ceiling. Antigua today is a rather sleepy town, well known as the craft centre of the island. There is an annual *feria* that concentrates on arts and crafts, and a regular craft market. The local cultural centre trains young people in the traditional music and dance of the island.

From Antigua, head westwards on the FV30 towards Betancuria. The road goes over a pass, from where there are fine views at the **Mirador de Morro Velosa** looking

LIFE IN THE DESERT

It might be thought that a barren place such as Fuerteventura should be largely devoid of wildlife, but this is not the case. The island's shoreline, particularly at migration time, can be rich in gulls and wading birds. The dunes and barren gravel plains are home to a variety of desert birds, more typical of North Africa. These include the houbara bustard, the black-bellied sand grouse, the cream-coloured courser and the trumpeter bullfinch. Mammals are almost non-existent, with the notable exception of the introduced ground squirrel, which is thriving on the island.

Above: *Betancuria's charming church was consecrated as a cathedral in 1426.*

The monument on the side of Mount Quemada is a statue of **Miguel de Unamuno y Jugo** (1864–1936). Unamuno was born in Bilbao in mainland Spain and became Professor of Spanish at the University of Salamanca. His poems and writings on philosophy and modern civilization were widely read in Spain, but his political observations offended the dictatorship of Primo de Riveras and led to his exile to Fuerteventura.

over the whole of the north of the island. From here the road drops down into the village of Betancuria.

Betancuria **

This idyllic village takes its name from the Norman conqueror **Jean de Béthencourt**. He landed on the west coast of the island, but became frustrated by the frequent raids of pirates. In 1405 he decided to push inland and set up his capital at Betancuria, where there was a permanently flowing stream, lush vegetation and a greater degree of security. It was to remain the administrative centre of the island for over 400 years. The village church, the **Iglesia de Santa María**, was consecrated as a cathedral in 1426, although no bishop has ever resided there. Betancuria's remote location proved no hindrance to pirates, however, and in 1593 a band of men led by the North African Jaban, attacked and set fire to the town, destroying the cathedral. It was not rebuilt for a hundred years. The cathedral has a beautiful wooden *Mudéjar* ceiling, made of wood from Tenerife and supported by delicate round stone arches. The *reredos* behind the altar is dripping with gold leaf and includes the Virgen del la Peña, the patron saint of both the town and the island. Look, too, for the bishop's head carved in wood and the *Last Judgement* painting by the baptistry in the southwest corner. The sacristy, to the left of the altar, contains some church silver and vestments. There is no organ in the church – nowadays it is more of a museum than a place of worship. Don't worry if you cannot gain immediate entry to the church – the lady curator who has the key commutes between the church and the nearby museum. On the far side of the small church square is the **Casa Santa María**, a restored town house that is now an excellent restaurant. There is a shop in the basement selling local ceramics and craft items.

Close by is a small **museum**, which has an excellent multi-vision show on the island of Fuerteventura. Among the displays are traditional agricultural implements, including ploughs, camel seats and harnessing, as well as a collection of local herbs and spices.

In the main street, on the far side of the normally dry river valley, is the town's **Museo Arqueológico**, which contains a number of archaeological finds from Guanche times. It is open from Tuesday to Saturday (10:00–17:00) and Sunday (10:00-14:00). On the northern edge of the town is the ruined **Convento de San Buenaventura**, a Franciscan monastery dating back to the early days of the Conquest. It closed down in the 19th century and much of its stonework was stolen for building material. There has been some restoration of the monastery's church, but it is usually locked up.

With more goats than people living on Fuerteventura it would be a pity not to visit a **goat farm**. There is a convenient one on the road a few kilometres south of Betancuria, which is very child-friendly. Here you can see goats in their indoor pens and watch them being milked, while ducks and chickens wander around the place. There is a small restaurant and shop, where the locally made goats' cheese and honey can be sampled.

Leave Betancuria northwards on the FV30, passing the Mirador de Morro Velosa and then turning along the **Valle de Santa Inés**. The valley, the village and its church were named after one Inés Peraza, who provided money for the church to be dedicated to the saint of her own name in the 16th century.

Head now along the FV207 towards the village of **Tefia** where there is an **open-air museum**. Old farm buildings and

> **GOATS GALORE**
>
> Foreign drivers in Fuerteventura are often surprised to see road signs warning them of the likelihood of cows or deer straying across the road. Surely a mistake? Yes. What the motorist should be looking out for are **goats**. However, there is no international road sign for a goat, so a cow or a deer motif has to suffice. There are reputed to be some 68,000 goats on the island of Fuerteventura and they are raised for the production of goats' milk, which is then made into cheese. Unfortunately, goats eat any vegetation and this defoliation of the island has contributed to the low rainfall resulting in increased aridity – a climatic vicious circle.

Below: *The entrance to one of the many goat farms on the island of Fuerteventura.*

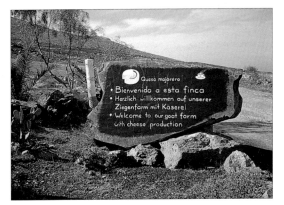

houses have been reconstructed and reassembled here, along with restored windmills, straw 'ice houses' and assorted ovens – all funded with EU money.

Continuing north, now on the FV10, the road swings between two mountains. On the right is **Montaña La Muda**, which at 689m (2260ft) is the highest mountain in northern Fuerteventura. On the left we see **Montaña Quemada**, which rises to 294m (964ft). This is the site of the **Monumento a Don Miguel de Unamuno**, the poet and academic who was exiled to Fuerteventura for many years in the early 20th century.

La Oliva *

The tour now approaches the town of **La Oliva**, yet another of the inland settlements that has served as capital of Fuerteventura. It dates from the early 17th century when it was a residence for the island's governors. Sadly, many of the town houses from those times seem in need of renovation. Dominating the town is the parish church of **Nuestra Señora de Candelaria**. Its square tower of dark volcanic rock contrasts strongly with the white-washed walls. Inside there is a *Mudéjar* ceiling and some interesting paintings. Of the numerous town houses, the most impressive is the **Casa de los Coroneles**, which was the home of the island's military governors and dates

Below: *One of many goat farms on Fuerteventura, where it is said that there are more goats than people.*

from 1708. Look over the main door at the coat of arms, which belonged to the Cabrera-Béthencourt family, descendents of the original Norman conqueror of the island. Opposite the Casa de los Coroneles is the **Centro de Arte Canario**, based in another town house, the Casa Mané. The paintings here are modern, as are the sculptures, which are displayed in a courtyard.

Above: *A needlewoman at work in the embroidery school at Lajares.*

Continue northwards to the village of **Lajares**. As the village is approached, the attention is drawn to two well-preserved windmills dating back to the 19th century. On the right is a more substancial 'male' *molino* (mill), while on the left is the more flimsy timber structured 'female' *molina* – making an interesting comparison. Lajares is also famous for its embroidery. Next to the windmills is the **Artesania Lajares**, where it is possible to watch women at work embroidering and lace-making. You can buy their products at the shop.

If you have enough time, a diversion can be made from Lajares to the west-coast fishing village of **El Cotillo**. Once noted for its smuggling activities, El Cotillo has recently been discovered by tourists. There are some good fish restaurants around the old harbour, which is the most picturesque part of the village. The only monument of interest is the **Castillo del Tostón**, just to the south of the port. It was built in 1743 to help repel the medley of pirates who plagued the coast. The fort is round and tapers skywards. Originally, troops lived on the ground floor, while the upper level was used for water storage. There has been some renovation, and the castle is open to the public. From El Cotillo, return to Lajares and head back to the ferry at Corralejo on the FV109 and the FV101.

JEEP SAFARIS

Off-road tours by jeep are not common in Lanzarote because of the amount of protected land, but in Fuerteventura they are a common excursion option for tourists. These four-wheel-drive vehicles can cover rough volcanic terrain, usually out of bounds to normal cars, but remember that open-top jeep safaris can be hot, windy and uncomfortable. Despite the term 'safari', don't expect much in the way of wildlife on these trips, as Fuerteventura has few mammals and only a small number of bird species. The scenery, however, is magnificent and the emphasis is on having a good time. Choose a reputable company with reliable vehicles.

Northern Fuerteventura at a Glance

BEST TIMES TO VISIT

Fuerteventura is an all-year-round destination, with not a great deal of climatic variety. If any rain falls it will be during the winter months, when the evenings can be cool. Summers are hotter, drier and windier.

GETTING THERE

Although it is possible to fly from Arrecife to Puerto del Rosario, the short distance and the expense involved do not make this a very sensible option. Most visitors from Lanzarote take a ferry, either from Playa Blanca to Corralejo or from Arrecife to Puerto del Rosario.

GETTING AROUND

Many visitors are taken around to explore northern Fuerteventura on a coach excursion. Others prefer to bring their own hired car over with them from Lanzarote. Another possibility is to come over on the ferry as a foot passenger and hire a car once in Corralejo. Either way, visitors find driving conditions convenient and similar to those in Lanzarote, with clear signposting and good road surfaces. Scooters and motorcycles can also be hired in Corralejo, as can mountain bikes for those who have a more limited budget or more adventurous inclinations.

WHERE TO STAY

As most visitors from Lanzarote are on a day trip, accommodation is usually not considered. It is quite possible, however, to come to the island for a few days, and the advice then would be to book accommodation well beforehand, particularly at the more popular times of the year.

LUXURY

Hotel de Fuerteventura, Playa Blanca, Puerto del Rosario, tel: 928 851150, fax: 928 851158. Severe looking building, but with all the comforts one expects in this former *parador*.
Tres Islas, Carretera Grandes Playas, Corralejo, tel: 928 535700, fax: 928 535858. This is probably the best hotel on the island, with a beachfront location in the beautiful natural park.

MID-RANGE

Rui Oliva Beach, Playa Corralejo, Corralejo, tel: 928 535700, fax: 928 866154. This is a family-friendly hotel with an Olympic-sized pool, situated right on the beach.
Hotel La Posada, Calle María Santana Figueroa 10, Corralejo, tel: 928 867344, fax: 928 536352. A conveniently centrally placed hotel with a roof terrace and a swimming pool.

BUDGET

Hotel Corralejo, Calle Colón 12, Corralejo, tel: 928 535246. Budget establishment favoured by windsurfers. Centrally located and on the beach.
Hoplaco, Avenida Generalisimo Franco, tel/fax: 928 866040. Simple apartments with pleasant gardens.

WHERE TO EAT

LUXURY

Hotel de Fuerteventua, Playa Blanca, Puerto del Rosario, tel: 928 851150. Pricey, but genuine, Canarian food, as well as an international menu.
Casa Santa María, Plaza de la Iglesia, Betancuria, tel: 928 878782. One of the best restaurants on the island. Atmospheric, but quite expensive.

MID-RANGE

For good seafood in Corralejo, try the following restaurants along the waterfront: **Marquesina I** and **II**, **Sino Juan**, **El Frio de Pescador** and **Sotovento**. All are good!
La Barca, Avda. Generalisimo Franco, Corralejo, tel: 928 866054. Another good seafood restaurant.
El Rincon de Perico, Calle General Linares 40, Corralejo, tel: 928 535722. A good range of tradional Canarian dishes and unusual *tapas*.

Northern Fuerteventura at a Glance

Fogelera, at the northern end of Avenida Maritima, Corralejo. Cheap, cheerful local restaurant with views across to Isla de los Lobos. **Vicoletto**, Calle la Ballena 6, Corralejo. Cheap pizzeria near the harbour.

Tours and Excursions

Most travel agents in Lanzarote arrange coach excursions around northern Fuerteventura, visiting **Corralejo** (but not Puerto del Rosario), **Antigua**, **Betancuria** and **Lajares**, as well as a goat farm. Tours can also be arranged from Corralejo, both around the north of the island and out to **Isla de los Lobos**. Contact Ultramar Express, Hotel Rui Oliva Beach, Corralejo, tel: 928 866251. For personal **taxi tours** of the north of the island, contact Autos Estupinan, Avenida Generalísimo Franco 18, Corralejo, tel: 928 866048. Other possibilities include dune walks, boat trips and deap-sea angling. For **jeep safaris** contact Unisafari, Avenida Generalisimo Franco 18, Corralejo.

Further South: As Fuerteventura is only 100km (62 miles) in length, it is perfectly possible for day-trippers from Lanzarote to see something of the south of the island. This is particularly easy with a hired car. South of

Puerto del Rosario is the resort of **El Castillo**, which boasts an old fort, a yachting harbour and an attractive sandy bay. Not to be missed is the charming fishing village of **Tarajalejo**, with good seafood restaurants and a noted art gallery. The major resort in the south is **Jandia Playa**, with impressive white sand beaches. Inland, the main settlement of note is **Tuineje**, an agricultural village with a Moorish feel.

Useful Contacts

There are **Tourist Information Offices** at: **Puerto del Rosario**, Avenida de la Constitución 5, tel: 928 530844. Open from Monday to Friday (08:00–14:00). There is also a kiosk at the airport that is open daily (09:00–20:00).
Corralejo, Plaza Grande de Corralejo, tel: 928 866235. It opens from Monday to Friday (09:00–13:00 and 16:30–19:30). There is also tourist information available at the ferry port.
Ferry services: contact **Naviera Armas**, tel: 928 867080. Their vessel *Volcan de Tindaya* leaves Playa Blanca at 09:00, 11:00, 17:00 and 19:00. It leaves Corralejo at 08:00, 10:00, 14:00 and 18:00; **Fred Olsen Line**, tel: 928 535090. Their ship, the *Buganvilla*, leaves Playa Blanca at 08:00, 10:00, 14:00, 16:00 and 18:00. It leaves Corralejo

at 09:00, 11:00, 15:00, 17:00 and 19:00. Crossings take approximately 35 minutes; tickets for the shipping services are not interchangeable. **Trasmediterránea** runs a ferry service between Arrecife and Puetro de Rosario; there are three services a week and the journey takes three hours. For more information tel: 928 811188 (in Arrecife) and tel: 928 850877 (in Puerto de Rosario).
There is plenty of opportunity for **water sports** at Corralejo: for **diving**, contact Dive Centre Corralejo, tel: 928 866243; for **windsurfing**, contact Flag Beach Windsurf Centre, and for **deep-sea fishing**, contact Pez Velero, tel: 928 866173. For **car hire** services, contact Cigar, Centro Comercial Atlántico, Avda. Generalísimo Franco, tel: 928 866413, and **Hertz**, Avda. Generalísimo Franco 84, Corralejo, tel: 928 866259.
For **motorcycles, scooters** and **mountain bikes**, try Mal Fun Club, Avda de Juan Carlos 1, tel: 928 535152.

Shopping

Craftwork typical of Fuerteventura can be found in a number of places in the northern part of the island. Artisans can be seen at work, for example, at the **embroidery** school in Lajares. Also highly recommended is Casa Santa María in Betancuria.

Travel Tips

Tourist Information

The **Spanish Tourist Board** has offices in the USA, in Canada, in Australia and in a host of non-English-speaking countries. In the United Kingdom, the address is: Spanish National Tourist Office, 22/23 Manchester Square, London, W1M 5AP, tel: 020 7486 8077, fax: 020 7486 8034, 24-hour request line: 0900 1669920, website: www.tourspain.co.uk Other websites which provide additional information include: www.icanarias.com www.lanzarote.com www.lanzarote-fuerte.com and www.okspain.org On Lanzarote itself, the tourist authority is based at the government offices, Cabilda Insular, Blas Cabrera Felipe, 35500, Arrecife, tel; 928 810118, fax: 928 800080. The main tourist information office in **Arrecife** is on the waterfront at Avenida Generalisimo Franco 6, tel/fax: 928 811762. They supply maps, brochures and advice on accommodation. The office is open from Monday to Friday

(09:00–13:00 and 17:30–19:30), and on Saturday (09:00–13:00).
At **Puerto del Carmen** the tourist office occupies a distinctive octagonal wooden building on the seafront in Avenida de las Playas, tel: 928 513351. Open from Monday to Friday (09:00–13:00 and 17:30–19:30) and Saturday (09:00–13:00). There is also a small tourist office at **Playa Blanca**, situated near the ferry terminal, tel: 928 517794. It is open from Monday to Friday (10:00–18:00).

Entry Requirements

Visitors from Britain, USA, Canada, New Zealand and Australia must have a valid **passport**. If staying for longer than three months a **visa** is required from the Spanish Embassy in their native country. Anyone losing their passport should contact their consulate. Most of these are in Las Palmas, but the British Consulate has a representative at Hotel Los Fariones in Puerto del Carmen during the months of February, May, August and November.

Customs

The Canary Islands, despite being part of Spain, are not considered a member of the EU. The European Union abolished the duty-free allowances in 1999, but at the time of writing certain limits remain on goods taken in and out of Lanzarote. There are advantages and disadvantages. For example, there are still bargains to be had at the airport's duty-free shop. The restrictions on the **duty-free allowance** are one litre of spirits; two litres of fortified wine and two litres of table wine; 200 cigarettes or 50 cigars; 60cc of perfume or 250cc of toilet water; and gifts up to the value of £145 sterling.

Health Requirements

No vaccinations are necessary unless coming from a country with smallpox, typhoid or yellow fever. There is no malaria in the Canary Islands and mosquitoes, while not entirely absent, are usually rare. Visitors from EU countries should bring **Form E111** with them, as it affords a degree of free medical treatment, although it is no substitute for a good medical insurance.

Getting There

By air: Cheap charter flights run to Lanzarote from many European countries, both from their main airports and small regional airports. There are no **scheduled flights** from northern Europe to Lanzarote. It is possible, however, to fly to Madrid and pick up an internal flight to Lanzarote. These flights are operated by Iberia's subsidiary Aviaco. An alternative would be to take a scheduled flight to either Tenerife or Gran Canaria and then an inter-island plane. All flights to Lanzarote land at **Arrecife Airport**. Note that a large number of charter flights arrive on a Thursday, making this a very busy day at the airport, with common baggage handling and check-in delays.

By sea: The only ferry (for both car and foot passengers) from Europe to Lanzarote is operated by Trasmediterránea (tel: 928 811019). It sails from Cádiz on the Spanish mainland and runs twice a week calling in at Santa Cruz and Las Palmas before proceeding to Arrecife on the return journey. Book well in advance for summer sailings.

What to Pack

With such a mild climate throughout the year, there is no need to pack heavy clothing. A light jumper and wind-proof jacket are useful during the evenings or if trips

to the breezier northern part of the island are planned in the winter months. For beach holidays, some light sandals are recommended as the volcanic sand can become very hot underfoot. Stronger footwear is needed for hiking over the volcanoes and badlands. The sun can be strong throughout the year, so sunglasses and a hat are advisable. Don't forget sun protection cream, and remember that light cotton clothes are most comfortable. Shorts and swimming costumes are essential. Smarter casual wear is needed for the evenings, particularly in the hotels and more expensive restaurants. Beachwear is unacceptable when visiting churches. *Lanzaroteños* themselves generally dress casually, except on more formal occasions. Lanzarote, with its clear light and stunning scenery, is a highly photogenic island and most visitors will want to bring a camera or camcorder. Spare films are readily available.

Money Matters

Currency: The Euro was introduced in January 2002. It is split into 100 cents. Coins come in denominations of one, two, five, 10, 20, and 50 cents, and 1 and 2 Euro coins. Notes are issued in five, 10, 50, 100, 200 and 500 Euros.

Currency Exchange: Travellers' cheques and foreign currency can be cashed at banks, exchange outlets and hotels. Remember to have your passport available. There are automatic cash dispensers

---

ROAD SIGNS

Traffic symbols in Lanzarote are those used throughout the EU and they are internationally recognized. The road signs include:

Alto • Stop
Camino Cerrado • Road Closed
Cedo el Paso • Give Way
Circunvalación • By-pass
Curva Peligrosa • Dangerous Bend
Derecha • Right
Derecho • Straight On
Despacio • Slow
Dirrumbes en la Via • Rock falls on the road
Dirección Unica • One Way
Izquierdo • Left
No Adelantar • No Overtaking
No Estacionar/Parquero • No Parking
No Hay Paso • No Entrance
Peligro • Danger
Reduzca Velocidad • Reduce Speed
Salida • Exit
Semáforo • Traffic Lights
Trabajos en la Via • Roadworks

(ATMs) in all the main resorts, in a variety of languages.

Banks: Finding a bank is not a problem, although service may be slow. They are open on weekdays from 09:00 to 14:00 and on Saturdays from 09:00 to 13:00.

Credit Cards: The major credit cards are accepted throughout Lanzarote in most shops, hotels and exchange offices (but not at all restaurants).

Tipping: A service charge is added to hotel and restaurant bills, so tipping is a matter of personal choice.

Accommodation

Most of the accommodation on Lanzarote is geared to package tours, which means that the individual traveller who just turns up might find hotels and apartment blocks fully booked. It is best to arrange accommodation before arriving on the island. There is a vast range of **hotels** from luxury establishments to modest *pensiónes*. **Aparthotels** have similar facilities, but have some self-catering rooms. **Apartments** far outnumber hotels and are cheaper, but beware that prices may be per room, even if not fully occupied. ***Pensiónes*** are in short supply, apart from a handful in Arrecife, and the island is not really a good location for the independent budget traveller. ***Casas rurales*** are converted farmhouses or village properties that make an attractive option for those who wish to get away from the bustle of the large resorts.

Eating Out

A wide range of **restaurants**, especially in the main resorts, provide for every need and palate. The resort restaurants cater mainly for tourists and therefore provide international food. There are usually printed menus posted outside the premises, often with a national flag representing each language, and in some cases photographs of the various dishes. Fast-food restaurants abound, such as KFC, McDonalds and numerous pizza outlets. Restaurants specializing in food from Italy, Thailand, India, France, Mexico and many other countries ensure that the visitor has a wide choice. To experience genuine Canarian food head inland, away from the large resorts, or to the capital Arrecife. One of the joys of eating out in the Canary Islands is to sample food in the many **seafood restaurants**, which provide a variety of fresh shellfish and fish, usually at reasonable prices. **Cafés and bars** are found everywhere and many provide ***tapas*** with drinks. A cheap way of eating is to order the meal of the day (*menu del día*), which usually consists of a starter, main course, dessert and a drink.

Transport

Air: There are inter-island flights from Lanzarote to all the other Canary Islands. Airlines include Binter, Spanair and Canarias Regional Air.

Ferries: All the islands in the group are served by regular ferry services, run by Compania Trasmediterránea, Lineas Fred Olsen and Naviera Armas.

Buses: Known by the South American name *guaguas* (pronounced *wahwahs*), the buses provide a patchy service around the island.

Car Hire: Car-hire rates on Lanzarote are just about the cheapest in Europe and with a good, well-signposted road system the rental of a car can add much to the enjoyment of a holiday. Most of the international rental firms have an office at the airport and also deliver vehicles to hotels. Drivers should be careful, as there are a large number of hire cars on the roads of Lanzarote and a dawdling convoy of such cars can drive local drivers to distraction when they are trying to get to work. Although there are many (often complex) roundabouts on the island, it is a curious fact that there are no traffic lights whatsoever!

Driving hints: In Lanzarote you drive on the right, overtake on the left and give way on roundabouts to traffic coming from the right. Carry your driving licence and passport (or a photocopy) when driving, as the police can demand to see them. Seat belts should be worn at all times, including those in the

CONVERSION CHART		
FROM	**TO**	**MULTIPLY BY**
Millimetres	Inches	0.0394
Metres	Yards	1.0936
Metres	Feet	3.281
Kilometres	Miles	0.6214
Square kilometres	Square miles	0.386
Hectares	Acres	2.471
Litres	Pints	1.760
Kilograms	Pounds	2.205
Tonnes	Tons	0.984
To convert Celsius to Fahrenheit: x 9 ÷ 5 + 32		

rear seats. It is prohibited to use a mobile phone when driving and it is also forbidden to throw objects out of the windows. Police can impose on-the-spot fines to non-resident drivers, but there is a 20 per cent discount if the fine is paid immediately. Speed limits are 120kph (75mph) on motorways, 100kph (70mph) on dual carriageways, and 90kph (55mph) on other roads. There is a speed limit of 60kph (35mph) in built-up areas. **Parking** can be difficult in Arrecife and the larger resorts, where parking meters and pay-and-display areas are marked by blue lines. **Petrol stations** are widespread along the main roads of Lanzarote and the majority accept credit cards. Fuel is cheaper than in the mainland and the rest of Europe. It is advisable to have a good map of Lanzarote if driving around the island. The *Globetrotter Travel Map* that accompanies this guide is recommended. **Taxis:** Lanzarote's taxis are good value by European standards. They are generally modern Mercedes and show a plate with the letters SP (*servicio publico* – public service). They are metered for short journeys, but for longer trips you should negotiate the fare with the driver. A green light means the taxi is free for hire.

Business Hours

Offices, post offices and most shops are open between 09:00 and 13:00, and, after the siesta period, between 16:00 and 19:00. On

Saturdays opening hours are from 09:00 to 13:00. Food stores and supermarkets (*supermercados*) may open for longer periods, while some shops in the tourist resorts may open on Sundays.

Time Difference

Lanzarote, along with the rest of the Canary Islands, maintains Greenwich Mean Time in the winter months, so there is a one-hour time difference with the continent. Clocks are one hour ahead in summer.

Communications

Telephones: If making an international call from Lanzarote, dial 00 first, then the country code, followed by the area code (omitting the first 0) and then the number. If dialling Lanzarote from abroad, the country code is 34 – the same as the rest of Spain. There are plenty of distinctive blue telephone booths, which take both phone cards and cash. These cards (*tarjetas telefónicas*) can be bought at post offices, tobacconists, shops and hotels. If making long-distance calls, it is best to use the large cabins or *locutorios*. You pay on leaving and credit cards are accepted.
Post: Post boxes (*buzons*) are yellow in colour. Stamps (*sellos*) are sold at post offices (*oficinas de correos*), tobacconists (*estancos*) and shops that sell postcards. Post offices open during normal office hours. Allow a week for a card to reach the Europe, 10 days to North America and two weeks for Australia, New

Zealand and South Africa.
Fax: Most hotels provide a free fax service, but expect to pay a fee for the service in a post office, tourist information centre or Internet café.

Electricity

The electric current is 220 volts for shaving sockets. Plugs have two round pins in line with most of Europe. Bring adapters for appliances and buy them before leaving home, as it is unlikely you'll find them here.

USEFUL PHRASES
Yes • *Si*
No • *No*
Please • *Por favor*
Thank you • *Gracias*
Hello • *Hola*
Goodbye • *Adios*
See you later • *Hasta Luego*
My name is... • *Me Llamo...*
Do you speak English? • *¿Habla (usted) Inglés?*
You're welcome • *De nada*
I don't speak Spanish • *No hablo Español*
How much is...? • *¿Cuánto cuesta...?*
Do you have...? • *¿Tiene...?*
Please speak more slowly • *Hablé más despacio, por favor*
Where is...? • *¿Donde está...?*
What time does it arrive/leave? • *¿A qué hora sale/llega?*
It's too expensive • *Es demasiado caro*
Do you have anything cheaper? • *¿No tiene algo más barato?*
Is there...? • *¿Hay...?*
Please fill the tank • *Llénelo del todo, por favor*
Is there a hotel near here? • *¿Hay un hotel por aqui?*

Weights and Measures

The metric system is used in both Lanzarote and the rest of the Canary Islands.

PUBLIC HOLIDAYS

The following public holidays are **fixed dates**:

1 January • New Year's Day (*Año Nuevo*)
6 January • Epiphany (*Epifanía*) or Three Kings' Day (*Día de los Reyes Magos*), when children are given presents.
19 March • Saint Joseph's Day (*Día de San José*)
1 May • Labour Day (*Día del Trabajo*)
30 May • Canary Islands Day (*Día de las Islas Canarias*)
25 July • Feast of Saint James the Apostle (*Día de Santiago Apóstol*)
15 August • Assumption Day (*Asunción*)
12 October • Day of the Spanish-speaking World (*Día de la Hispanidad*)
1 November • All Saints' Day (*Todos Santos*)
6 December • Constitution Day (*Día de la Constitución*)
8 December • Feast of the Immaculate Conception (*La Immaculada Concepción*)
25 December • Christmas (*Navidad*)

In addition there are a number of **movable feast days**. These are Maundy Thursday, Good Friday, Easter Sunday, Whitsun, Ascension Day, and Corpus Christi. Note that Boxing Day, Easter Monday and Whit Monday are not public holidays in Lanzarote. In addition, there are a number of **regional fiestas** that are also local holidays. Consult the local tourist offices for full details.

Health Services

Citizens of EU countries are entitled to free medical treatment on production of Form E111, which should be obtained before travelling. This form does not cover medical prescriptions or dental treatment. Lanzarote has some good hospitals and a host of private clinics with English-speaking staff. Hotel receptions usually provide the name of an English-speaking doctor (*medico*). Minor medical problems can usually be solved by visiting a pharmacy (*farmacia*). *Farmacias* are open during normal business hours and are distinguished by a green cross. In the larger towns at least one pharmacy will be open after hours and a duty rota is displayed in the window.

Health Precautions

Most visitors to Lanzarote experience few health problems. The biggest danger is over-exposure to the sun, resulting in **sunburn** and **dehydration**. Sunbathing should be taken steadily and sunblocks should be applied generously. Wear a sun hat and good sunglasses – avoid exposure during the hottest parts of the day. Note that sunburn is possible even if there is a layer of cloud.

Personal Safety

Crime is relatively low in Lanzarote, even in Arrecife. Local authorities realize that adverse crime figures can affect the tourist trade, which means that the police keep a high profile in order to keep the island safe. Most visitors will not feel threatened at any time, but nevertheless petty crime does exist.

Emergencies

For the **police**, call **091**. For **medical** emergencies requiring an ambulance, call **062**.

Etiquette

Topless sunbathing is common at beaches and around pools, but full nudity is frowned upon and is only tolerated in certain remote locations, such as the Papagayo beaches. Beachwear is not acceptable when visiting churches.

GOOD READING

Concepción, José Luis (1984) *The Guanches – survivors and their descendents.* A sympathetic account of the early inhabitants of the Canary Islands. Ediciones Graficolor, La Laguna, Tenerife.
Fernández-Armesto, Felipe (1982) *The Canary Islands After the Conquest.* A specialized history of the islands in the 16th century. Clarendon, Oxford.
Sánchez-Pinto, Lázaro and de Saá, Lucas (1993) *Flora of the Canary Islands.* A handbook and map in folder form. Ediciones Turquesa, Santa Cruz, Tenerife.
Walker, Ann and Larry *Pleasures of the Canary Islands: Wine, Food, Beauty, Mystery.* Particularly good on cooking. Hardback.
Clarke, Tony and Collins, David (1996) *A Birdwatcher's Guide to the Canary Islands.* Prion, UK.

INDEX

Note: Numbers in **bold** indicate photographs